Presented in conjunction with the
Forty-Ninth Anniversary

Evening of Celebration of

ישיבה דרכי תורה
YESHIVA DARCHEI TORAH

Motzoei Shabbos, January 8, 2022

Honoring

Mr. and Mrs. Chaim and Bracha Schulhof

Guests of Honor

Mr. and Mrs. Jake and Rochel Walden

Parents of the Year

Mr. and Mrs. Motti and Yael Guttmann

Kesser Shem Tov Award

Mr. and Mrs. Shumy and Rivkah Reichmann

Hakoras Hatov Award

Rabbi and Mrs. Shimon and Chanie Dachs

Leadership in Chinuch Award

Special Presentation recognizing
Rabbi Joel Beritz

Mr. Menachem Marx   Mr. Nesanel Goldman

Dinner Chairman   Journal Chairman

ArtScroll® Series

Rabbi Nosson Scherman / Rabbi Gedaliah Zlotowitz
General Editors
Rabbi Meir Zlotowitz ז״ל, *Founder*

Chinuch

Published by

ArtScroll
Mesorah Publications, ltd
in conjunction with

**Yeshiva
Darchei Torah**

THE JOSEPH EDITION

RABBI YAAKOV BENDER

for Today

A veteran mechanech answers pressing questions

FIRST EDITION
First Impression … January 2022

Published and Distributed by
MESORAH PUBLICATIONS, LTD.
313 Regina Avenue / Rahway, New Jersey 07065

Distributed in Europe by
LEHMANNS
Unit E, Viking Business Park
Rolling Mill Road
Jarow, Tyne & Wear, NE32 3DP
England

Distributed in Australia and New Zealand
by **GOLDS WORLDS OF JUDAICA**
3-13 William Street
Balaclava, Melbourne 3183
Victoria, Australia

Distributed in Israel by
SIFRIATI / A. GITLER — BOOKS
POB 2351
Bnei Brak 51122

Distributed in South Africa by
KOLLEL BOOKSHOP
Northfield Centre, 17 Northfield Avenue
Glenhazel 2192, Johannesburg, South Africa

ARTSCROLL® SERIES
CHINUCH FOR TODAY
© *Copyright 2022, by* MESORAH PUBLICATIONS, Ltd.
313 Regina Avenue / Rahway, New Jersey 07065 / (718) 921-9000 / www.artscroll.com

ITEM CODE: CFTH
ISBN 10: 1-4226-3028-5
ISBN 13: 978-1-4226-3028-0

Typography by CompuScribe at ArtScroll Studios, Ltd.
Printed in the United States of America
Bound by Sefercraft, Quality Bookbinders, Ltd., Rahway, N.J. 07065

This volume is dedicated in memory of our dear grandparents

Rabbi Asher and
Mrs. Daniela Chaya Buxbaum ז"ל

ר' אשר בן יצחק
ודניאלה חיה בת החבר שלמה ז"ל

Refugees from Germany, they met shortly after the war in Montreal, where Zeidy, an alumnus of the Gateshead Yeshiva, received *semichah* from Rav Elya Chazan and founded a chapter of Zeirei Agudath Israel.

It was not the norm to study in kollel in the 1940s, yet Zeidy and Bubby became one of the pioneer kollel couples in America when he joined Rav Aaron Kotler's Beth Medrash Govoha in Lakewood. With very little in the way of material possessions, they devoted themselves with *mesiras nefesh* to serving Hashem and studying His Torah.

Despite a university degree which could have gained him entrée into a panoply of professions, Zeidy chose to devote his life to *chinuch*. Both in the classroom and as a principal, he left an indelible impression on generations of students throughout his career, all of whom could not help but be enriched by his sterling character and integrity, his tangible connection to his Creator—most evident during *tefillah*—and his lifelong *hasmadah* in Torah.

Bubby, who cherished her primary roles as a wife and mother, was a paragon of *kibbud av va'eim* to her own parents. In fact, she treated *all* people with dignity and respect. Her *tefillos* and *berachos* were always said with focus and concentration and she took pride in preserving the Yekkishe mesorah of her forebears. A protégé of Mike Tress *a"h*, she was a founder of Camp Bnos and a lifelong volunteer and officer for N'shei Agudath Israel, a post from which she succeeded in enhancing the lives of countless needy families in Eretz Yisrael and America over the course of six decades.

Zeidy and Bubby enjoyed great *nachas* from the Torah-true family that they raised together on American shores. Their personal examples continue to inspire their children, grandchildren and great-grandchildren to follow in their beautiful ways.

Mendy and Tzipi Joseph

Table of Contents

All in the Family

Money Matters

Choices, Choices — Selecting the Right School for Your Child

Developing Daveners

Reward and Punishment

In the Classroom

Out of the Classroom

*I*n a Social Forum

Specific Circumstances

When Something is Amiss ....

A Matter of Faith

Middos, the Measure of Man

When an Ex Is Involved

Yesomim

Foreword

Our people are blessed with visionaries, who see what is and what can be and dedicate their lives to achieving it. Rabbi Yaakov Bender is a visionary. He saw his calling in being *mechanech* Jewish children, bringing out the best in them and offering them the chance for a brilliant future.

Our people are blessed with builders. Rabbi Yaakov Bender is a builder. He began by building children, and today he builds people of all ages, from kindergarten through elementary school, high school, *cheder*, *mesivta*, *kollel* and beyond. He gives people self-confidence, belief in themselves, and the tools they need to excel in life.

He also builds buildings, edifices in which his spirit hovers over each room, where love, life, Torah and education thrive. The buildings are testaments to his trailblazing leadership in *chinuch*. The buildings impress by their outward beauty and grace, but those who know what goes on within their walls appreciate that the beauty of the Torah that is studied there and the students who do the studying far outweigh that of the gleaming, handsome, impressive structures.

When Rabbi Bender moved to Far Rockaway and joined the staff of Darchei Torah, it was a small boys' school in a quiet suburban community. As word spread about who Rabbi Bender was and what he was accomplishing, the school and the community began its rapid ascent. Soon, Rabbi Bender added a *mesivta*, and then a *yeshiva gedolah*, and ultimately he added a *kollel*. In the process, the community blossomed into an *ir v'eim b'Yisrael*.

The visionary and builder that he is, Rabbi Bender created the need and filled it, building an empire of Torah in the process. Through it all, he has not lost sight of what makes him great and sets him apart. Rabbi Bender cares about every Jewish child. He cares about each child reaching their potential. He loves every boy in the school and nothing stops him from working to ensure that every person in Darchei Torah reaches their potential.

Every person is created differently. Everyone has a different mission to fulfill in life. Rabbi Bender is attuned to that and works to ensure that each student receives the love and care he needs to establish a firm and enduring foundation of knowledge and comportment necessary to lead a productive, effective, and successful Torah life.

Every one of Rabbi Bender's *talmidim* is fortified with *middos tovos*, self-assurance, and a healthy amount of self-respect and belief in his own ability to excel in learning. Enormous resources are dedicated to forming happy, healthy, proper *bnei Torah*. Beginning with the morning greeting, every person a Rabbi Bender *talmid* encounters throughout the school day treats him the way we all wish we were treated when we went to school.

Rabbi Bender represents the best of the world of *chinuch*. He understands children, teenagers, and parents. He appreciates their challenges and motivations and is able to relate to them. That, coupled with his inner, deeply felt love, Torah knowledge, and concern, enables him to deal with the multiple issues that crop up on a regular basis, and provide assistance and direction, setting and keeping people on the path of positivity and growth.

Rav Bender demonstrates daily that optimism overcomes negativity. He epitomizes through what he has been able to accomplish that a person who sets himself on the proper path and works *l'sheim Shamayim* without ulterior motives is empowered with *siyata diShmaya*. Thus, he is renowned worldwide as an effective leader and Rosh Yeshivah who enables thousands to grow and blossom in the vineyard of Hashem.

Thanks to his vision and superhuman efforts, he has not only built great edifices of and for Torah, but he has filled them with diligent *talmidim* and provided them with devoted, enthusiastic rebbeim, as well as roshei yeshivah and administration members to lead the flourishing operation and ensure that the mission remains the same as the yeshivah continues its remarkable growth. He has also developed a cadre of dedicated *baalebatim*, who are blessed with Rabbi Bender's infectious vision and express their appreciation and optimism for the future as they invest in Rabbi Bender and the Torah *chinuch* he provides.

In Darchei Torah, Rabbi Bender created an island where Torah is accessible to all. Not only are the needs of the gifted students addressed, but those of the weaker students are front and center. The yeshivah also accommodates students with impairments who wish to be taught Torah, despite their wheelchairs, hearing aids, or poor communicative abilities.

Thousands of families in Far Rockaway and the Five Towns have benefited from Rabbi Bender, as he has influenced their lives and provided them with the ultimate in Torah *chinuch* and education. We all owe him a debt of gratitude for what he has accomplished, enhancing the world of Torah and *Yahadus*, providing leadership and direction in a world of *hester*, where there are so many pressures and temptations vying for our attention and time.

In this book, as in his previous publications, Rabbi Bender teaches, shows, cajoles, prods, and inspires us to grow and be as good as we can be.

May Hashem continue to shower His blessings upon Rabbi Bender and his family as he helps prepare the world for the coming of *Mashiach tzidkeinu. Amein.*

Rabbi Pinchos Lipschutz
Editor and Publisher, Yated Ne'eman

Introduction

כָּל הַיּוֹם חוֹנֵן וּמַלְוֶה וְזַרְעוֹ לִבְרָכָה.

All day long he is gracious and lends,
and his children are a blessing.
(Tehillim 37:26)

Once, when Rav Chaim Avraham Orenstein, a close talmid of the Chasam Sofer, came into his room, his rebbi shared his anguish. "I am busy from early morning until late at night with my talmidim and the kehillah — when shall I tend to my own family?"

Reb Avraham replied by quoting the above pasuk, which refers to a righteous man and the reward for his generosity, but he interpreted it homiletically... The reference is to a tzaddik so generous and compassionate, that "kol hayom, the entirety of his day," is given to others. He listens and encourages and guides and teaches. He's a chonein u'malveh with his most precious commodity — his own time. As a reward, Hashem assures him that "za'ro livrachah, his own children — to whom he cannot fully dedicate himself — will be blessed in Torah and fear of Heaven."

(*Adapted from* The Chasam Sofer, *by Yisroel Besser*)

Serving in the world of *chinuch* is undoubtedly one of the most satisfying and gratifying privileges that one can imagine.

It can be overwhelming, especially in terms of the time invested — many *mechanchim* are forced to live above time, as it were, with few hours in the day or evening that can truly be called their own. They have little time to spend with their families. Yet Hashem watches over them and their loved ones. As the Chasam Sofer and other *gedolim* have taught us, there is a special *berachah* bestowed upon those who devote their lives to the *klal*, ensuring that their progeny will remain true to the path of Torah.

We are living in an era when many sages, whom we relied upon for advice and guidance, left this world within a short span of time, and there is an undeniable void. Parents are thirsting for answers as they navigate the often-choppy waters of *chinuch habanim*. I find that the period we are living in now is the greatest in terms of the sheer quantity and intensity of *nisyonos* — more so than at any time in my 40-plus years of *chinuch*. The Covid-19 pandemic did not help in this regard; we have new challenges and new issues to address, many of which do not seem to be going away in the near term. The damage to people in many cases has been permanent, whether it be the lingering physiological effects known as "Long Covid," families that have been torn asunder or lost *parnassah*, and seemingly-permanent negative effects on the mental health of both young and old.

The temptations for today's children are incredible. It can be argued that it has never been more difficult for someone to develop into a real *ben-* or *bas-Torah* than it is today. And yet, there have never been more *bnei Torah* than today! Torah is flourishing all over the world.

This is not a dichotomy; those who have the *cheishek, hasmadah, bren* and wherewithal, and are living in functional homes, are thriving. Others are struggling. The letters in this *sefer* bespeak many of these issues.

Granted, there are a lot of special-education programs and schools set up for children with challenges, but most of these youngsters long to be a part of the "regular" system.

This *sefer* looks to be *mechazek* all families — and the afore-mentioned ones in particular: You are heroic, you are normal, you are healthy, and we as *mechanchim* have a responsibility to reach out and help you.

When I was a fresh *yasom* at Brooklyn's Mirrer Yeshiva, my rebbeim there understood what it was like for me, because they themselves had arrived in America after World War II without families and with few possessions. Rav Shmuel Berenbaum *zt"l* once said to me, "*Ir veis vos es meint? Nisht kein tatte, nisht kein mamme, nisht kein brider, nisht kein shvester — gornisht!* Do you know what it means [to survive] without a father, without a mother, without brothers and without sisters — with nothing?" Reb Shmuel became one of the greatest roshei yeshivah America has ever seen — and he was not only a giant in Torah, he was also soft, sweet, and a thoroughly beautiful personality. So while there were so many people around us in the 1950s and 1960s who were broken, they all *understood* "broken." (Perhaps that is why the Mirrer yeshivos — both in America and in Eretz Yisrael — are anything but elitist. If you want to learn Torah, you are welcome there.) The leaders of the great Mirrer *oilam*, who in large part transplanted the Torah of Europe to America, were battered and broken — and they reached out to American boys to give them a *geshmak* in Torah. Many of these boys came from backgrounds completely devoid of Torah knowledge or ideals, and these *Alter* Mirrer brought the *geshmak* and beauty of Torah to them.

Rav Mendel Kaplan *zt"l* became one of the greatest *marbitzei Torah* after the war, first in Chicago and later in New York and Philadelphia. Rav Berel Wein recalls how Reb Mendel arrived in the classroom on his first day, initially unable to speak English, and opened the *Chicago Tribune*, asking the boys to translate the news to him in Yiddish but then proceeding to "translate" it back to them by showing them the meaning hidden between the lines. His entire career as a *maggid shiur* was in that vein, reaching his *talmidim* at their level with love and joy, despite having lost almost his entire family.

Just this past Shabbos, Reb Moshe Benoliel, a *talmid* and a member of the yeshivah's executive staff, showed me a beautiful thought from Rav Meir Zlotowitz *zt"l*, who wrote that perhaps the reason why Yaakov Avinu finally acquiesced to his sons' plea that he send Binyamin down to Mitzrayim only when Yehudah made the request, was because Yehudah, having buried two children of his own, understood his father's pain as no one else could. (Yaakov was still under the impression that his son Yosef had passed away and feared that he was about to lose Binyamin as well.)

Was there ever another *manhig* in America of the caliber of Rav Moshe Feinstein, *zt"l*? A few years ago, I went to the *bris* of a son of one of our *kollel yungeleit*, Rav Eli Winzelberg. It was there that I met his late grandfather, who told me over his own story. Mr. Elozor (Louis) Palgon *a"h* was born in Tarentum, Pa., a small town near Pittsburgh. When he and his brother reached late childhood, their father decided that they must go to New York to learn in a yeshivah. The senior Mr. Palgon was brokenhearted when he could not gain them admission. Having failed in his quest, he was about to return to his hamlet when someone told him that there was a great Jew, Rav Moshe Feinstein, on the Lower East Side of Manhattan who had only recently arrived in America. "Go see him," they advised. He walked into the *beis medrash* of Mesivtha Tifereth Jerusalem on East Broadway and noticed a short, older man standing on a back bench, straightening out *sefarim* on the bookshelves.

Mr. Palgon asked the man: "Do you know where I can find Rav Moshe Feinstein?"

Reb Moshe turned to him and replied, "How can I help you?"

He said, "I have two boys here and I need to find a yeshivah for them."

"*Nu, geit oiben un registrirt zei* — Just go upstairs and register them."

Today the Palgon descendants are all *ehrlich, frum Yidden*, and count among their ranks many *marbitzei Torah* in addition to Reb Eli Winzelberg, who is a huge *talmid chacham* — because Reb Moshe *zt"l* understood what it means to help someone.

Besides Rav Shmuel Berenbaum *zt"l*, my other rebbeim at the Mir were so *mekarev* me: Rav Elya Jurkanski, Rav Shraga Moshe Kalmanowitz, Rav Shmuel Brudny, and the *mashgiach* Rav Hirsh Feldman, *zichronam livrachah*. When I became engaged nearly all of them traveled to my *vort*, and I believe almost every one of them spoke there as well. I still remember what they said and the *chizuk* I got from them at the time. When my wife and I made our first *bris* on Erev Rosh Hashanah, they all came, and they all spoke! (Yes, it was very late by the time the *bris* ended.)

In addition to the *maggidei shiur* I had at the Mir, I had other great rebbeim who treated me so wonderfully as well: At Torah Vodaath, I had Rav Yisroel Belsky *zt"l* — who was not only a rebbi but a best friend — and Rav Yitzchok Karp *zt"l*, who typically focused on out-of-town students who knew no one, but with whom I was lucky to have a close relationship as well. The way he treated his own developmentally delayed son, Yisroel Meir *a"h*, was a lesson to all of us *talmidim*.

Our job as parents and educators is to reach out and touch the lives of the children in our charge, no matter who they are, and even if — nay, *especially* if — they are growing up in a broken or dysfunctional home. We must welcome them into our yeshivos with one mantra in mind, as Rav Elya Svei *zt"l* always used to enjoin us: "*Vos vil di Eibishter fun unz* — what does Hashem want from us?" In the same vein, Rav Shmuel Kamenetsky, *yibadel l'chaim tovim va'aruchim*, constantly urges us to take care of every single child in *Klal Yisrael*.

I was so fortunate to have spent my childhood summers at a bungalow colony in the Catskills together with today's Rosh Yeshivah of Beth Medrash Govoha, Rav Aryeh Malkiel Kotler. It is a friendship we never lost, and I am the richer for it. His parents, Rav Shneur and Rebbetzin Rishel *zichronam livrachah*, were so *mechazeik* my mother *a"h* as an *almanah*, and I am grateful that my friendship with Reb Malkiel endures as a *kesher kal kayama*.

Rav Elya Brudny, a Rosh Yeshivah at the Mirrer Yeshiva, is more than a visiting *maggid shiur* at our yeshivah; he is a *yedid nefesh* who helps me see the light on so many issues. *Klal Yisrael* is lucky to have a person of his stature and *chochmah* in the vanguard of its leadership.

Serving on the Vaad Roshei Yeshivah of Torah Umesorah is an exceptional experience for me. Being in the presence of such august *talmidei chachamim*, led by Rav Hillel David, as well as leaders of the caliber of Rav Dovid Nojowitz and Reb Zvi Bloom, is an indescribable *zechus*.

My mother, Rebbetzin Basya Bender *a"h*, was my best friend. After my father Rav Dovid *zt"l's* sudden and untimely *petirah*, I was compelled to return home from out-of-town yeshivah and stay with my mother. Only 15 years old, I thought to myself, *my life is over.* But that seven-and-one-half-year period with my mother as my confidante, mentor, and best friend was, in hindsight, the best thing that ever happened to me.

My wife, Rebbetzin Bryna Minna *shetichyeh*, is wise, intelligent, and intuitive — where would I be without her? Baruch Hashem, she keeps me grounded. Each one of our wonderful children, *bli ayin hara*, is a constant source of *chizuk* to us.

HaKadosh Baruch Hu has allowed me to work in a *makom Torah* alongside some of the most capable and dedicated *mechanchim* in the world. The Rosh Yeshivah, Rav Shlomo Avigdor Altusky, holds all of us to a high standard. The various *menahelim* ensure that Yeshiva Darchei Torah continues to be a place where every child is given the chance to be a *gadol b'Yisrael*. The staff and *baalebatim* of the yeshivah are exceptional, and I am grateful for the opportunity to work with them.

At Yeshiva Darchei Torah, I am privileged to enjoy the material and moral support of many giants of Torah philanthropy and *achrayus* to the *tzibbur*, most notably my *chavrusa* Mr. Yehuda (Ronnie) Lowinger, Mr. Aryeh Leib (Lloyd) Keilson, Mr. Motty Klein, Mr. Avi Weinstock, and Mr. Yaakov Sod. May they, their families, and all the loyal pillars of Torah chinuch be *gebentched* for all time.

The dedicator of this book is my close *talmid*, Reb Mendy Joseph. Mendy and his wife Tzipi continue to bring *nachas* to all of his rebbeim as well as to their parents, as they raise their own children to follow in their ancestors' glorious footsteps, *al haTorah v'al ha'avodah*. I am eternally grateful for their gift, one that will continue to bear fruit for many years to come.

The letters that comprise this book — and many more that remain unpublished — came to me over the last few years; I did my best to respond to each of them and we chose those exchanges that we thought would benefit the wider public.

The contribution of this volume's editor, Mrs. Ilana Keilson, has been invaluable. She organized my correspondence, deftly refining and upgrading it into the present form while remaining faithful to the original.

Reviewing a manuscript is yeoman's work, and I thank my son Rav Dovid Bender and son-in-law Rav Yehoshua Rosenberg for going through every page with the proverbial fine-toothed comb, ensuring that the final product is indeed fit to print.

Observers may think that I write all of my own articles and emails; I certainly do. But I am grateful to have Reb Moshe Benoliel at my side to assist me on various written projects; I am the richer for it.

Rav Pinchos Lipschutz, the trailblazing founder and editor of *Yated Ne'eman* on these shores, gave me my start in chinuch writing when he invited me to join the *Chinuch Roundtable*; I will forever be in his debt. I am thankful to Rav Yisroel Besser, an eloquent *talmid chacham* and communicator who helps me write my *sefarim* on *Chumash*.

Rav Gedaliah Zlotowitz is not only a worthy successor to his father, Rav Meir Zlotowitz *zt"l*; he is forging his own new and exciting paths in Torah literature and I am grateful for his trust and his friendship. May he and Rav Nosson Scherman continue enriching *Klal Yisrael* until and including *Yemos HaMashiach*.

The entire ArtScroll team has been a pleasure to work with, particularly Mendy Herzberg, who shepherded this project; Eli Kroen, who designed the cover; and Mrs. Judi Dick, Mrs. Estie Dicker, and Mrs. Esther Feierstein, whose expertise in developing this book is evident throughout.

May this book help to enrich the lives of our heroic *mechanchim* and parents, and may we all march together soon to greet Mashiach, experiencing the fulfillment of וכל בניך לימודי ה׳ ורב שלום בניך.

Yaakov Bender

Far Rockaway, New York
Teves 5782

Chinuch Begins at Home

Chinuch Guidelines

Q *n general, what is the mehalech in how to be mechanech our children in a pleasant manner?*

A We must not pressure children to do anything. It is a major reason why kids rebel. Do it only with *gutskeit*. If you drive kids crazy, you are taking a big risk.

I once asked Rav Aharon Leib Shteinman if I am ever allowed to expel a student. He said absolutely not. I asked what if he hurts other kids. He said then throw out the whole yeshivah.

You must *keep* your guidance age-appropriate. Be very careful.

A couple came to me to express dissatisfaction at the *trop* and *havarah* that is used in the first grade. Another family expressed disappointment that their three-year-old child was playing with battery-operated toys on Shabbos. Another couple complained that their three-year-old doesn't wash *netilas yadayim*. These are all age-inappropriate. You must always consider the age of the child.

The Mother's Role in Chinuch

Q *I am a teenaged girl and I am wondering: What is a woman's role in chinuch? What advice do you have for a teenaged girl who wants to eventually become a good mother b'ezras Hashem?*

A A mother is the key to *chinuch*. It starts and ends with her. Fathers generally do not spend as much time with their children. It is the mother who does the job. *Chinuch* starts the moment a mother is expecting. When a woman is expecting, she should take good care of her health and daven that everything should be well for this child during pregnancy and beyond. *Chinuch* is not just giving lessons over to the child, but more importantly, the daily goings-on in the home. Even babies pick up on these things. Everything a mother does is picked up by her child. A mother must realize that her children will imitate all that she does. That does not mean she has to be "super holy," but *ehrlich* and a real *mentch*. As for advice for a teenaged girl, become an *ehrliche* young woman and everything else will fall into place.

Find the Middle Ground

Q *My husband and I have slightly different approaches when it comes to the chinuch of our children. In general, I feel that our children need a softer approach, together with boundaries, while my husband is more "old school" and feels they need a stronger, more disciplined approach. Recently he was very abrupt with one of the kids, who ended up hurt and upset. I tried to give my husband my opinion on the matter when we were out of earshot of the kids.*

How can I convince my husband that the kids need a softer touch (they are all under bar/bas mitzvah) without his thinking that I am not machshiv his way of doing things? My husband feels very strongly that we can't raise a child to be a kafui tov or lacking in middos and derech eretz. I agree with that sentiment, but I think the way of achieving it should be different.

We do not argue in front of our children, and our home is one of peace (or as peaceful as it can be with seven young, lively children!). We are on the same page about most things, but this area definitely creates some strain in our relationship. We both know how important shalom bayis is for the children and we are both committed to strengthening our shalom bayis. I am just unsure how to best navigate this.

Do I go along with my husband and follow his ideas of stronger discipline and then on my own shower the kids with extra love, or do I continue to try to convince my husband that they truly need a softer, more loving way? Will that make him feel undervalued and that he can't get it right in dealing with the kids?

Please understand that in general, my husband is soft-spoken. He loves the kids, but wants them to toe the line. He plays with them often and they have a lot of fun together. But he is also a sensitive person and he takes the kids' remarks personally, which doesn't help his handling of them.

My husband himself was brought up in a bit of a rigid environment. His parents had very high expectations of him and his siblings. He also comes from a small family. I, on the other hand, am one of fourteen, so I am definitely used to more chaos than he is.

A You are both correct! You must find the middle road. In any event, you should not tell your husband how you feel. If anything must be said, you must find someone he respects to tell him to be a little softer.

As an *eitzah tovah* to you, kids are very resilient. They can take *mussar*, even when they don't deserve it. Sometimes it is important for the disagreeing parent to look the other way. Don't see everything as something that will make or break your child. If you clearly see that your husband's *hanhagah* is creating kids who are uptight and feel unappreciated, then you should do something. However, if the only problem is that YOU don't like it, *nisht geferlech* (it is of little importance). Your job is to make sure your home is a happy place. Right now, it seems that you are not happy, and it is important for you to be happy. Work it out together. But as long as your kids are happy, do not shake up the world.

Motivation in Mitzvos

Q However hard I try to motivate him, my twelve-year-old son does not daven at all and does not bother bentching after he eats. He is not the brightest boy, and when it comes to doing chazarah on Shabbos, he always refuses to learn with me. Last Shabbos, he did agree to learn with me. Of course, I did everything I could to make it geshmak and enjoyable, but after just two minutes, he was totally not interested.

I have always been easygoing with him, never demanding anything from him, instead just showering him with love. I am wondering if what I am doing is the correct approach. Perhaps I should try something different?

A It is very difficult to attempt to analyze such a situation in letter form, without knowing the details and history of the young man. Rest assured that each issue you mention by itself is very commonplace.

However, here we have a number of different issues. *Bentching*, *chazarah*, and davening are all areas with which young adolescents may have a hard time. And there are *eitzos* that may work. But I am afraid that we are talking about a young man with a major motivation problem. I will attempt from afar to find some kind of solution.

You make a passing reference to the fact that "he is not the brightest boy." For a parent to say this, it might mean that we have a large issue with *kishron*. If that is the case, you need to work on somehow giving the child a feeling of success in his learning. Twelve years old is a bit late. How many poor tests has this child already been through? How many feelings of failure has he already experienced? This child needs a very great dose of self-confidence. Take him to a specialist in building up children to find a way (and quickly) to make this young man a brand-new person.

May you have much *hatzlachah*!

Appropriate Reading Material

Q *I know chinuch is by example. What are some good books/sefarim to learn with my children to help them navigate this tumultuous world?*

A Good books are about *gedolei Yisrael* and also about men and women, such as Moshe Reichmann and Rebbetzin Kanievsky, who are wonderful role models. The best way for them to learn is through osmosis.

Easing Up on Restrictions

Q *My children are constantly complaining that I stifle them and don't allow them to do any of the things they would like to do. My boys want to watch baseball games and my girls want to watch movies. They are always asking for iPads and things like that. As of now, I have* *been pushing them off or telling them no. I send them to regular, mainstream yeshivos and Bais Yaakovs. Unfortunately, this is where they may have picked all this up.*

My husband and I grew up in more modern homes. I grew up with secular videos, music and television. I so badly want my children to be better than this and not grow up with these influences, as I have worked so hard to rid myself of these things.

My oldest, a thirteen-year-old girl, has already vocalized that we are too yeshivish for her, and she wants to do things that we wouldn't. My twelve- and ten-year-old sons get very upset when we don't give in.

We do try to fill our home with fun and happiness and we try to have nice Shabbos seudos and fun outings and vacations. How do I find a balance here? Or should I stay strong and continue to say no in a loving way?

Your question is one I receive constantly. It is a very difficult question to answer. You have every right to insist that the children not have internet access. However, especially in these Corona times, you must give in a little bit. There are kosher movies they can watch. iPads can be TAGGED and filtered. Find a way to walk the middle road. *Iy"H*, you will do very well. Once school restarts, put more limits in place.

Eliminating Boredom

My eldest son is in sixth grade. He comes home from yeshivah at around six p.m., and as he is getting older, he is staying up later. Lately, during the evening, he becomes bored. He does read, but not for four hours every night. After eating dinner and sharing a bit about his day, he has little to keep him occupied now that the weather is cold and he cannot ride his bike or play ball with his friends.

A Get him a *chavrusa* twice a week. You should also start a program to help him finish *mishnayos* for a bar mitzvah *siyum*. Give him a prize for every two *perakim* he finishes, with each succeeding prize ascending in value. At the end of a *masechta*, take him out for a special dinner. Be a little bit creative.

And keep encouraging the reading! It is the key to success for all learning in school.

Violent Games Are Not the Answer to Boredom

Q *My son is thirteen and in eighth grade. He is very bored and restless after school. He learns on a good level, baruch Hashem, but is not very motivated and is not interested in doing extra learning or the like after school. He keeps asking me for things to do, but rejects all my suggestions (woodworking, learning a musical instrument, etc.). He also does not like sports. He asked me to ask Rabbi Bender if he can play a certain game. He is baruch Hashem self-aware that too much gaming is not good for him, as it makes it harder for him to fall asleep. During the lockdown last year, I did allow Zoom for Night Seder America and other games that we selected on an iPad, but I took that away when school reopened, and he was completely on board with that. But now, he is incessantly complaining about boredom and asking for this.*

A Certain things, I believe, have no compromise. Some games, like the one you mentioned, are *sakanas nefashos*. Under no circumstances should you allow your son to play such games. There are endless ways to fill free time. Keep exploring your options. Once he understands that this is not something you will give in on, he will be more open to choosing another pastime. If you must allow gaming, make sure it is on a safe device and choose pareve games together.

Sticking With Chalav Yisrael

Q My son is in camp and he keeps telling me how hard it is for him that he is the only one in the bunk who doesn't eat chalav stam. Should I let him eat chalav stam only in camp?

A Tell your son that all of us are tested once in a while. This will build his character and his spiritual strength. It is important not to give in.

This is not a question of yes *chalav stam* or no *chalav stam*. While I personally ate *chalav stam* till I became a teenager, based on Rav Moshe Feinstein's *psak*, there was really almost nothing available in *chalav Yisrael*. But I don't understand why people who live in the NYC metropolitan area don't keep *chalav Yisrael* nowadays. It boggles my mind when we visit people and they offer us coffee but they don't have *chalav Yisrael* milk. Years ago, it may have been a lot more expensive, but not today. Some people still have a bug that *chalav Yisrael* doesn't stay fresh that long. Baloney!

We use only *chalav Yisrael* in our home, and it lasts quite long. Every type of chocolate bar, *milchige* candies, and ice creams are available today in *chalav Yisrael*. Why not do what is optimal? He will survive in camp. And there are plenty of *chalav Yisrael* items available in camp canteens.

Supervised Online Shopping

Q My sixteen-year-old daughter wants to be able to shop online. Though in the past, I have taken her to my office to do such things, she wants to be able to do it from *home. As of now, my younger children (under eighteen) do not have access to internet in the house. I do have filtered internet for my older children, though. How should I handle my sixteen-year-old's request?*

A I would allow her to use the computer at home provided it is in a communal area and you keep an eye on her. Under those conditions, it is not an issue. However, you must be sure that your filter keeps out non-*tznius* images.

Acting Out Requires Therapy

Q *I am having a very hard time with my twelve-year-old son. He has deteriorated to the point that he goes to school, gets asked to leave class within the first five minutes, then spends the rest of the day wandering the halls. And this is with a very dedicated rebbi who has been bending over backward trying to help him.*

My son's behavior is purposeful. He wants to show that he isn't listening. He wants to show that he is in control. He is very angry at everyone and everything. He will purposely knock Yiddishkeit and anything frum.

I want to help him, but I don't know how.

A I am sorry to say that this is beyond the scope of being solved by me. Has he been to a therapist? Your son needs intensive therapy before any other steps can be taken. But please don't give up. This is a phenomenon we see regularly with young teenagers. With the right therapist, you shall overcome!

Playing Ball Is Not Shabbosdig!

Q *Most of the boys our son plays with on Shabbos are playing ball with bats and mitts. We feel that is not appropriate for Shabbos play. At what age do we make an issue about this, especially as the parents around us do not seem to have an issue with it?*

A This problem has been haunting us. Times are changing and it is a terrible problem. I agree with you: ball playing is not for Shabbos, regardless of the presence of an *eruv*.

However, there are still many parents who do not allow their children to play ball outside on Shabbos. I don't think you should be afraid to teach your children that this is not something we do. Every family must make its own *ruchniyus* rules. I am not saying we should ban this, but to you I say, *chazak chazak v'nischazeik!*

Personally, I am a bit bothered with this issue. This problem was not around years ago. Kids, no matter how young, knew that certain things are just not done on Shabbos.

One doesn't ride a bike on Shabbos, one doesn't play ball on Shabbos, one doesn't ride a scooter on Shabbos, and on and on! Where have we gone wrong in all of this? As a child we used to go to Pirchei on Motza'ei Shabbos for learning and their playroom, and we didn't change into our weekday clothing. Today Shabbos is missing something. Why not play some old-fashioned board games? We must finally all step up — from rabbanim to roshei yeshivah — and try to put a stop to the near-*chillul Shabbos* going on.

Ball-playing on Shabbos

Q *What is the right age to begin to disallow ball playing outdoors on Shabbos?*

A Truth be told, no children should play ball outside on Shabbos, no matter what their age (excluding very small children who cannot play organized sports anyway). Certainly a father should not be playing ball with his kids. Unfortunately, times dictate certain things. Today, in almost every neighborhood in New York and New Jersey, kids are playing ball on Shabbos. However, I would make certain age limits. By the time a child enters middle school, he should not play ball on Shabbos. He will say everybody does it, but you will say, "Sorry. We don't." At younger ages, you can remind them that Motza'ei Shabbos will come soon enough and they can play then.

Ban Guns, Not Dinosaurs

Q *I have read in many places that it is not good to let our children play with dinosaurs because many concepts connected to them are not for a Jewish home. I also wanted to ask about gun play. Are all guns bad, or are water guns okay?*

A You can let him play with dinosaurs. Today, dinosaurs are innocent. Guns are much worse. My children were not allowed to play with any guns whatsoever. There are plenty of water-spraying toys that are not guns. It should be understood that guns are not for a *Yiddishe* child.

Battle Toys and Battle Stories

Q Our son is requesting certain toys such as ninja and superhero Lego sets. He sees such things in his friends' homes. Are these in the same category as guns, or are they okay? At the same time, he loves parashah stories and stories from Navi and he specifically requests war stories from David HaMelech and the like. Is it okay to read him such things?

A I have always felt that guns are not proper toys for Yiddishe children. Guns belong to Amalek. They are the "yadayim yedei Esav." That being said, they are not similar to the ninja turtle-type toys. It's hard to differentiate between the two, but I do feel that ninja turtles and such similar toys are looked upon by kids as just that — toys! But even a fake gun brings out the worst in children. When they play with guns, it becomes all about killing people. They will actually even scream out, "I will kill you!"

Regarding the stories of David HaMelech, you should absolutely not read them to him if the reason he wants to hear them is because of the "blood and gore." However, if you are reading stories from Tanach to him and these will just be some of many, then it is perfectly fine. It would be helpful if you, as a parent, explain to your son that the wars of David HaMelech were not what we think they were, but were part of *milchemes mitzvah* and the *ratzon Hashem*. This is not very different from the explanation one must give young *talmidim* when teaching the *Akeidah*. It is important for children to understand that we cannot relate to or judge our forebears in Tanach, as they were on an infinitely higher level than we are. I have no doubt you will manage to present things in the right way.

Boys and BB Guns Do Not Mix

Q My twin sons, who are fourteen, bought a BB gun behind our backs. As soon as we discovered it, we of course confiscated it immediately. This was during Corona when they were both home and bored and needed some fun. But we felt a BB gun was crossing a line. The boys were furious and it took them a long time to get over it.

Now, one of them is baruch Hashem learning and shteiging in an out-of-town yeshivah and doing very well. His twin, however, is homeschooled. Unfortunately, he saw a neighbor with a gun, shooting animals. He is furious that we won't let him get one as well, threatening to get one behind our backs again. He is a good kid in general, not into any other things that concern us. I don't know how else to tell him NO! I am also concerned that when his twin comes home during bein hazemanim and faces summer boredom, he will be dragged into this again. Shouldn't this be a legitimate no? A battle that we should pick?

A First of all, you have a right to say, "WE DON'T ALLOW GUNS. PERIOD." There are black-and-white issues; this is black and white. Parents have a right and even a responsibility to draw a line. Guns do not belong in a *Yiddishe* environment. The fact that others do it means nothing. But I am afraid that you may have a bigger problem here than his just wanting something he cannot have, and he should see someone. You need to get your son back on the right track. A therapist would be very helpful. It will especially help vis-à-vis his twin brother, who will see that the issues that his twin is involved in brought him the need to go to therapy.

Healthy Interest in Construction

Q Our eleven-year-old son is fascinated by the construction site near our home and spends many after-school hours there, chatting with the workers and watching what they do. We're not sure how to proceed. He really loves what they do and likes watching each detail, and I think that's healthy. However, it is true that the language of the workers is hardly what we would want our child exposed to. How should we proceed?

A Everyone is created differently. People have different talents, mindsets, and needs. *HaKadosh Baruch Hu* ensures that those who have issues in one area are able to excel in other areas. Your son obviously enjoys construction. Good for him! Who knows if it will come in handy one day for him? Not every boy fits into the same mold. We should never stifle our children, unless they are getting into an area where they can be hurt long term.

I assume your son is a typical yeshivishe eleven-year-old. He knows right from wrong. He has heard people curse. Unfortunately, even if he is in the best environment, he has likely heard such words. He ignores it. He will not pick up anything bad from construction workers by watching them from a distance, even though he may occasionally hear some coarse words. The only time you have to worry is if he hangs out with them on their lunch break and shmoozes with them. That would be an *avlah*.

But observing people doing the type of work he likes is something you should admire. As long as he is doing well in yeshivah and is a cooperative young man, let him do something he enjoys.

There was a *tekufah* when elite *mesivtos* in America demanded that their *talmidim* not play ball. They have all come around. In fact, some very *chashuve mosdos* insist that their *talmidim* play ball and get exercise. We want to raise healthy human beings. Stay away from the cookie-cutter mentality.

In our yeshivah, we have found a very interesting thing. We

have a very strong vocational program for those who do not fit into our intensive learning track. It is amazing to see how many of the boys from the learning track are also interested in learning carpentry and plumbing. One day, they will be a lot better than I — they will be able to build a *succah* on their own.

If we are going to constantly look over our kids' shoulders and ban everything, we will create rebels. Children sense when their parents worry all the time and that is the worst thing we can do.

Enjoy your *nachas*, and stop worrying.

Kosher MP3 Player Is Acceptable

Q *My twelve-year-old son wants an MP3 player with a radio. I am not so comfortable with this, but don't want to say no if this is what is considered normal.*

A Such an MP3 is standard for many *bachurim* today. They use it for *shiurim*, *shmuessen*, and kosher music. You cannot take away everything. Let him have it, but keep a close eye on things. Try to purchase one without a radio.

Inappropriate Phone Use

Q *Yesterday, I gave my eleven-year-old my phone to look at some pictures. Later that night, I noticed that he had been searching for some somewhat inappropriate things. How do I address this incident? Is there a specific talk I should be having with him as he enters his adolescent years?*

A What he did is very normal and natural. Unless it becomes a habit, you don't have to worry. Even look the other way. But if you are going to allow your children to use your phone unsupervised, even supervised, you must get it filtered by TAG.

Caught in a Lie

Q *My son wanted to be picked up from school, saying he wasn't feeling well. The nurse checked him and sent him back to class. After Minchah, he came back to the nurse and said he was dizzy and short of breath. I picked him up from school and asked him to tell me the real reason why he wanted to be picked up. He said that some kids had been bothering him. He said he had been selling cookies in school and the rebbi said to stop selling them. Some kids didn't believe that the rebbi said that and called him a liar. Later, he told me that the story was a bit different. He had been telling the kids he made the recipe himself (he did not) and some kids didn't believe him but some still did. He said he's not going to school until everyone forgets about it because it's going to be the talk of the class tomorrow. I asked him why he lied and he said because he wanted the attention. I said, "You know you got yourself into this. If you continue to lie, people will stop believing anything you say. You have to go to school. Maybe bring a cool toy and that will divert their attention." But he couldn't think of anything to bring. He insisted that he was not going to school the next day, or until this blows over. Am I headed in the wrong direction here? What is the correct thing to do?*

A You're handling it expertly. But you must notify the rebbi and morah. When kids get upset, you must let it pass. I am not sure if it would be such a terrible thing to keep your son home a day or two until he is comfortable that the situation is blowing over. He clearly realizes he did the wrong thing. He needs a bit of time. Kids have feigned illness to avoid school since the first school opened its doors. Kids have created businesses of buying and selling since the first school opened its doors.

He certainly did not do the right thing, but you need to hold his hand somewhat till he gets over what in his mind is a crisis. It will eventually pass. Children mostly forget quickly.

Circumventing the Rules Is Not a Good Idea

Q My eleventh-grade son has a filtered smartphone. He attends a day school with the official rule that the boys may not bring phones to school. However, most of the boys sneak their phones into school anyway, some with parental permission, some without.

The principal tries half-heartedly to take control of it, taking them away here and there, but then when the boy or his parents beg to have it back, he capitulates. Unfortunately, most of the rebbeim and teachers do not want to get involved in enforcing the rule. They do nothing when they see the phones being used.

My son does not bring his phone to school, but is getting pressure from the others to bring it and is being questioned as to why he doesn't. Please let me know your advice on how to handle this situation.

A I never like to advise people to break school rules. However, if indeed all the boys bring their phones to school, then let him bring his once in a while. But he must know that it is at his own risk and that he may have it taken away and that if that happens, you will not plead his case. The only way a school can stop this is by taking the phones away permanently. By not sticking to their guns, they are encouraging disobedience. It is out of your control.

Hoverboard Is Inappropriate

Q *My sixteen-year-old daughter wants a hoverboard. I don't think it is appropriate to use in the street, and I don't see the point of buying one just to use in the house. She says she will use it in a parking lot. But I don't think she should be using it outside the house at all.*

A Explain to your daughter that in your area, girls of her age don't do such things. She may argue that "everyone else has one," and that can be difficult to respond to, but there is something important to remember: the word "everyone" might be 4-5 kids. And second, you are obviously (and correctly) concerned about the image of a sixteen-year-old *frum* girl from a yeshivish family skating. And again you are correct. You must explain to her that she does not want to label herself as part of the element that has nothing to do but hang out in the streets.

Too Cool Is Not Cool

Q *Our fifth-grade son has always felt a need to be part of the "cool" group. Starting this year, we are seeing a big focus on his exterior and his need to be like the "cool" kids growing ever stronger. Recently, he asked for several things: deodorant, so he can "smell good"; a different style yarmulke (one that is not part of the school dress code); to cut his peyos short without anything behind his ears. (He threatened to do this himself if we don't have it done or do it for him.)*

Where should we be firm and where should we give in? Each little thing is not a huge issue, but I'm concerned that agreeing to these requests will further shape him into what he considers "not yeshivish." On the other hand, I'm concerned that if we do not give in, he will take matters into his own hands. He is chasing some boys who do not share our standards, as well.

This is a boy who is at risk of becoming at risk. These days, we see this with younger and younger boys. Firstly and most importantly, you must hire a *geshmak'e, leibedige*, cool personality who is also a *ben Torah* to mentor him. Officially a *chavrusa*, but he should also take him out to eat or for walks, etc. once in a while. He will be able to accomplish much more than you in these areas. As for what you can do, are you overly demanding on him in *frumkeit* areas? If yes, slow down. Never force-feed religion. He should have an allowance so that he has some spending money. His father must spend time with him, one on one, and not just for learning. He must bond with him as well.

As for his specific requests, I would not fight on the deodorant. The yarmulke is easy — we follow school rules. As for his *peyos*, try every which way to convince him not to do it, even if you have to bribe him. *Hatzlachah* in everything!

Child Staying Up on Shavuos Night

My son is ten years old and insists that he wants to come with me to learn all night Shavuos night. At what age is it appropriate to bring a child to learn all night, and does taking him take precedence over my being able to stay in shul all night as opposed to possibly having to take him home during the night?

You can bring him for an hour. If he insists on longer, add another hour or so. If he insists on all night, allow it. No kid ever got sick from this. Of course, he may fall asleep and have to be woken up to go home after davening, but from a *chinuch* and medical standpoint, it's fine.

When a child shows signs that he wants to do a *davar tov*, allow him. Even if he is not *l'sheim Shamayim*, so what? We know that he wants to tell his friends the next day that "I stayed up all night." Who cares? Eventually, he will grow up and be learning all night for the right reasons.

Buying a DS System

Q Our ten-year-old son has been begging for a handheld video game. He has badly wanted one for a while now. His friends at school mostly do not have such things, but many of his neighbors and relatives have one. There doesn't seem to be anything wrong with the content; we can choose the games and disable the internet. However, we are not excited about getting him one. We don't like how playing on a handheld device encourages seclusion, addiction, and "sitting in a corner" oblivious to the world around. An idea we had was to get a family DS that would possibly be less addicting, as it would not be his and would have to be shared. As of now, we don't have any electronics in the house. We have a laptop that is mainly used for work. Our son is a creative kid with many other hobbies. He loves playing sports, cooking, and woodworking.

We do want our son to have games and activities in our house so that we can host and keep our home a fun and inviting place for him and his friends. Although he has his heart set on a DS, we were thinking that it may be more prudent to get him a more interactive computer game such as the Wii or Nintendo Switch, which are played together with other kids (and obviously, have no internet). Additionally, it would be nice for him to have something to do during downtime that doesn't involve *parental involvement.*

With all this in mind, what would the Rosh HaYeshivah advise?

   A. Stay with the status quo and convey the message that this is not something our family does.

   B. Get the DS he has been begging for and so badly wants.

   C. Get a more interactive video game.

   D. A different approach or option.

A One thing is clear: you must allow him to have SOMETHING. You cannot *assur* everything. But there must be TIME controls. He cannot play every night, and on the nights he does play, not more than half an hour, unless you deem that he deserves or needs more on a given night.

Cartoons — Occasionally

Q *My wife and I don't know what to do about letting our children (ages two to ten) watch cartoons. On the one hand, we live in an area where many children are allowed to watch these things. On the other, our children go to a school where this is not the norm. We have decided that we allow such things only on vacations and outside the house, with limits. Is this a good psharah?*

A Absolutely. You have to learn when to say yes and when to say no. In general, use good judgment. If you are tough all the time, it will backfire. Just strive for normal, for the middle road.

Bar Mitzvah Boy's Leining Is Optional

Q My son is becoming a bar mitzvah in about one month. However, he is not prepared enough. He has some kriah and focusing issues, and unfortunately we got off to a late start, as this year was especially challenging for our family for a number of reasons.

We will b'ezras Hashem be making a nice breakfast for his bo bayom with his classmates and rebbeim at the yeshivah (which is what most boys here do on their bo bayom). He will get an aliyah on that day as well.

As we haven't made any final bookings yet, we wanted to ask if there would be any problem with us pushing off the Shabbos leining and kiddush by a few weeks. Is there a specific inyan about having the leining and kiddush right after the bo bayom?

A Not only is there no *inyan* about having the *leining* right after the *bo bayom*, there is no *inyan* for the bar mitzvah boy to *lein*, period. He does not have to *lein*. He should learn the *berachos* and have an *aliyah*. So you can certainly push it off. Please make sure that he will be getting an *aliyah* on his *bo bayom* or the first *leining* opportunity after his *bo bayom*.

Trust Must Be Earned

Q Our ten-year-old son loves to play games on the computer and we allow that as a privilege for his learning well with his tutor. Today he asked to play and we told him no. Later he asked if he can type some divrei Torah on the computer so we said sure! A little while later, my daughter walked into the room and he was playing a game. How do you think we should respond?

Tell him if he is not honest, you will not be able to trust him in the future. If it happens again, there are other steps to take. These are everyday occurrences in many homes, but it is important that your children know that you will not tolerate deceit. It is very advisable that your home computer should be in a communal area, where private tricks are not possible.

Consistency Will Overcome Chutzpah

Our eldest son, who is almost four, is very chutzpadig toward my wife and me. He thinks we're all equal and that whatever we say to him, he can say back to us. If he gets a negative answer, he has no problem responding, "Well, then I'll smack you in the face!" If we ask him to stop doing something, he simply says no. What should we do? Should we punish? Should we potch? We want to nip this in the bud before he gets any older.

Avoid *potching*. Send him to his room. Warn him that he will not get dessert or snacks. And do not give in. Carry out the punishment. You must be consistent, that is the key. He may scream for a couple of weeks, but then he will start to behave. *Chinuch* is all about consistency, and even the slightest weakness will be exploited by children. Parenting is not always easy, but with the aforementioned consistency, you will eventually take control.

When Will Mashiach Come?

Q All around us, people are talking about Mashiach and how he is surely coming now during this global pandemic crisis. The children are talking about it as well, and time and time again, they ask why he hasn't come yet. How do we respond?

A I tell all the rebbeim in my yeshivah not to dwell on Mashiach because if he does not come, the disappointment is terrible. Now that it has already happened, tell the children that even the greatest *gedolei Yisrael* had dates when they thought Mashiach would come and it did not happen. *Ani maamin*, yes, but we move on with life in the meantime.

All in the Family

Courteous Negotiations

Q *Is it okay for a child to negotiate with his parents? For example, if told to get ready for bed, may a child say, "Can I have five more minutes please?" or is this a lack of kibbud horim?*

A There is absolutely nothing wrong with this type of negotiation with parents. We don't want to turn our children into robots. If a child is reading or playing, they naturally want to finish. Aren't we adults the same way? We also negotiate with others. We negotiate with our spouses. We negotiate with our grandparents. We negotiate when we take the *afikoman*! Of course, children must learn how to negotiate respectfully. But if they have proper *derech eretz*, it is perfectly fine. That said, it should be clear that parents make the final decision.

They Need Therapy

Q I am a single girl with several married siblings. One of my sisters is married with five children ka"h. I go to her often and have a close relationship with her and her kids. She works full time to support her family and is constantly stressed out and overwhelmed. As her children grow older, I am observing the house becoming more and more tense and the children acting up more and more.

My sister is very organized and her husband helps with household chores and childcare and they have a good relationship. However, her oldest child was always very emotional and impulsive and has become more explosive. He causes my sister added stress and worry, and this in turn makes the whole family out of sync.

As a result, my sister and her husband have become even more controlling and don't display any trust in their kids. For example, they don't let any of the children kiss or touch their five-month-old baby for fear they will take it too far. This causes the kids to try to be very wild with the baby, especially when the parents are not watching. In trying to anticipate and prevent things from spiraling out of control, they are strict and say "no" to many of the children's requests. They love their children and try to give positive reinforcement, but the negative interactions far outweigh the positive ones. In addition, they reprimand me for how I interact with their kids if they feel I am not acting in accordance with their rigid perspective.

I have degrees in psychology and education, and though I realize that that is very different from actually being a parent, I feel that I want to help my sister with suggestions and ideas. But she becomes very defensive.

Based only on your own observations of the *matzav* at your sister's, the only way you can help is to get your sister and her husband to go for therapy together. You must use a lot of *chochmah*, and it must be apparent that you really mean it for their benefit. But if you really want to help, stay out of it with your degrees. You will create a huge conflict! If you cannot get it done quietly, you must not get involved because you will create more antagonism. See if you can get someone to convince them to go for family therapy, if you see no way out from future disaster.

The Aquarium, Not Broadway

My parents are coming to visit from out of town, and they want to take my daughters to Manhattan to FAO Schwarz. They also want to take them to a Broadway show and the aquarium.

We try to keep a low profile. Our kids are happy with bowling and the dollar store. How do I approach this issue?

I hear you very well. Please explain to your parents how you are raising your children and that this will not help you. However, you must allow them to take your children somewhere. You don't want your parents to be hurt. Nor do you want your children to feel that they are never allowed to go anywhere. The aquarium is an excellent choice.

Critical In-Laws

My wife and I are having trouble with my in-laws. When we tell them anything we are doing with our children, they criticize us. For example, when we took our children to the Museum of Mathematics, they said that must have been boring for children so young. When we go to visit them, they watch my children like hawks, making sure they don't drop anything or spill. They are constantly correcting their behavior whatever they do. My children are all under 8 years old. Is it reasonable to expect them to be perfect all the time?

A I don't know your family dynamics, but from the wording of your question it seems that your in-laws are out of line. Unless something egregious is taking place, grandparents should stand back and let parents do their job. If they don't want you to mess up their house, let them come visit you instead of the other way around. They are jeopardizing their relationship with both their children and their grandchildren.

Rabbi Avigdor Miller used to say that parents of married children and in-laws have two jobs to do: Keep your wallets open and your mouths closed!

The Right Way to Complain

Q *Where is the geder between letting children complain in a healthy way and rebuking them for doing so? We know that the dor hamidbar was punished for complaining, but if we would give our child what he wants every time he complained, we would end up spoiling him.*

A The *geder* really depends on whether he is kvetching because he likes to kvetch, or because he really feels pain. If he really feels pain, he has a need to complain, but in a *b'kavodig* fashion. When the *Yidden* asked what they would eat, that was fine. But when they ganged up on Moshe Rabbeinu and spoke nastily, that was a problem. In the same way, if a person complains to me about something happening in yeshivah, I have no problem so long as they speak with *derech eretz* and *mentchlichkeit*.

Dealing With ADHD and Anger Issues

 Our fourth-grade son has ADHD, some language difficulties in terms of perception and black-and-white thinking, and struggles with some social/emotional issues. We had him evaluated by an expert social worker who felt she was seeing results of trauma (possibly from when I was frequently not home due to a parent's terminal illness). She suggested that we first get him started in play therapy, and then when he gets to a certain point, to start him in language therapy.

Meanwhile, his behavior has taken a sharp turn for the worse. He is incredibly angry. He walks around growling, stomping, and breaking things. He is not cooperative and refuses to get up and ready in the morning, often making the whole family late to school and work. He is hurting our other children, both physically and verbally. Worst of all, he is refusing to take his medication.

Can you guide us in the right direction?

I think he needs more than just play therapy. He will need all kinds of therapy, but first and foremost he must go on some type of medication that will specifically address his aggressiveness. You do not say what kind of medication has been prescribed for him and that he refuses to take. This is not an uncommon story, where children who already had issues were hit double by Corona. I don't know if your pediatrician prescribes such medications or if you have to see a psychiatrist, but I believe the therapies will be much more effective if he is first placed on medication. Obviously, whatever medication you now have is not doing the job. Today the world of medication has become much better. There are many different types of medications and your doctor will find the correct one. Do whatever you must to get him to take the medication, and explain to him that it is to make him feel better as he clearly is not happy. Then you will *b'ezras Hashem* have some peace of mind in your home.

Strained Relationship With Teenaged Son

Q *Our fifteen-year-old son is a bright, creative, resourceful, and stubborn young man. In earlier days, he would sometimes have tantrums and I would have to chase him all around the neighborhood. We had him tested, but he has no official diagnosis, other than that he is stubborn. At his bar mitzvah, he did beautifully, leining, saying a pshetel, and making a siyum Mishnayos.*

In seventh and eighth grades, he began slipping — not doing his work, being disruptive at times, and later, even sleeping in and skipping school. In the summers, he loved the sports and activities in camp, but did not "shtel tzu" to the davening and learning.

By the time he entered high school, he was home more than he was in school, asking to be switched to the lower shiur. Worst of all, he acquired a phone without filters behind our backs. He refuses to participate in therapy. Our relationship with him has become strained at best. What should we do? What should we NOT do?

A There are no easy answers to this question; it is a very tough situation. If at all possible, hire a mentor who will spend time with him every single day. Officially, call him a *chavrusa*, but he should also be a mentor, taking him out to eat and listening to what he says. Unfortunately, parents may not be able to help in this situation. Major studies by top psychiatrists have found that between fifty and eighty percent of teenagers don't relate well to their parents. A majority are even embarrassed by them. *Frum* psychologists agree that the same is true in our *machaneh*. But finding a top-flight mentor can go a long way in ameliorating the situation. *Hatzlachah!*

Getting Ready on Time Is a Challenge

Q *My seventh-grade son is having a lot of trouble getting ready for school in the morning. His rebbi is also noticing a lack of motivation in school. He created an incentive program for him to improve his grades, but it does not seem to be making a difference. Recently, he refused to get ready one day and completely missed school. Later on, I withheld a privilege that he had been expecting. This, too, had no effect. Please advise me what I can do.*

A There is something called benign neglect. Sometimes, you must look the other way. *Chinuch*, in a way, is an art. I would call it the art of deal-making. I am *baruch Hashem* the proud father of seven boys and one girl *bli ayin hara*. When I saw that one of my sons did not want to go to yeshivah for Shacharis, I made a deal with him. Stay home today, but promise you will go the rest of the week.

Think about it for a minute. Why should a twelve-year-old boy want to get up for *minyan* at 6:30 a.m.? Take some advice from this old man. Your son is entering adolescence. Pick your battles, and mostly, look away.

Afraid to Go to Sleep

Q *My fifth-grader (age ten) has been going to sleep very late — some nights after 10:00 or 11:00. While she may occasionally have a lot of homework, I think she mostly likes to stay up with her older sisters (ages twelve and thirteen) after the younger children are asleep. As a family in general, we are not early to bed, but I am trying to encourage earlier bedtimes (for all of them!). I tried telling her and my other daughters what you said in your book should be the latest bedtime for children.*

Recently, she mentioned that a book her teacher is reading to them is very scary, and she thinks about it when she goes to sleep. Today she told me that some classmates were discussing if they would have nightmares from the story. I am beginning to think that she may also be afraid to go to sleep because she is afraid she will have nightmares.

A It is normal for children of that age to want to be up with their older siblings (as they call it today, FOMO) and staying up late on occasion for a girl that age is fine. However, no teacher in the world should be reading scary stories to the girls, and I think you should contact the teacher or the principal. In general, we should dissuade children from reading scary stuff. We want to avoid nightmares.

First Come, First Served — Or Not?

Q *Every Friday night, I bentch my children. My second to youngest doesn't like the fact that we go in age order. He wants to switch it around so he doesn't have to always be almost last. Is it okay to do so? Or is it preferable to do it in age order as I have been doing?*

A It is perfectly fine to switch the order around, especially considering the fact that this child seems to need it. However, the challah should be given out in age order. What I do with the challah is: first my wife, then the married couples, then a tray of cut-up pieces to the younger kids.

Child Using Own Kos and Menorah

Q What is an appropriate age to buy my nine-year-old son his own kos for Kiddush, as well as a nicer menorah? What about for my daughter, who is five?

A If your family has a *mesorah* or a *minhag,* adhere to it. Otherwise, I think your son should have an oil menorah already. *Kos* is up to you. Girls can use candle menorahs or even oil menorahs for as long as they want to light.

Facts of Life

Q My wife is due to have a baby soon. My four-year-old daughter thinks that we buy babies in the store. She has no idea that my wife is carrying a baby. I spoke with our pediatrician yesterday, and he said it is not healthy for her to think this way. He recommended that I explain to her, in an age-appropriate way, what will be happening. My wife doesn't think we should tell her. What is Rabbi Bender's opinion?

A I'm sorry to disagree with the doctor, but my opinion is that there is absolutely no reason to have to explain all this to a four-year-old. You have plenty of time for that and she will come around. You don't have to TELL her that you bought the baby in the store, but if she thinks so, that is perfectly fine. (Bottom line: Always listen to your wife!)

Broaching Sensitive Topics

Q I have a twelve-year-old son who is entering seventh grade. Someone gave me a pamphlet called "The Kedushah Talk" which gives guidance in explaining *inyanei kedushah* to kids. What would be the proper age to have this talk with him? He hasn't asked any questions yet, but I'm sure it will come soon.

A Stay far away. Though there are some who believe in this conversation taking place sooner rather than later, it is certainly not for a seventh-grade kid. Maybe in high school. There are major differing opinions on this matter, but this is the way we were raised by our parents. Generally, in these *inyanim* there are major risks when you talk to kids at too early an age. Many children are not yet developed, and this conversation can cause much bigger problems than had you not spoken to the young man at all.

Brother Hits Baby Sister

Q Our four-year-old son is very geshmak and, in general, a normal kid. The problem is, he is very, very rough with our two-and-a-half-year-old daughter. He hurts her intentionally all the time, both when we are looking and when we are not. We have tried punishing him, giving her treats when he hurts her, but he doesn't stop. What can we do?

A You are obviously not punishing your son in a way that he will feel it. A four-year-old must learn right from wrong. There is nothing wrong with a light *"petchel"* here and there. If it means going to bed without dessert, so be it. You must find something that will make him think twice. To each their own.

Not Happy to Have Stepsiblings

Q *Do I have to like my stepsiblings? They just landed on my head when my mother remarried.*

A No. You don't have to like them. In fact, you don't have to love anybody in this world. Your mother remarried and she deserves to have a life. She chose the father of your stepsiblings because she felt that she had a chance to have a good life with him, and maybe even provide you with a good stepfather. No one can replace your father, but your mother chose this man to be her new husband and perhaps, in some manner, to be a father to you. Your mother deserves a shot in life. You will get married one day, and will have a wonderful life. She deserves no less.

The bottom line is this: This is your life now. You have a choice to either hate your life and give your mother a lot of grief, or try to figure out a way to learn to live with each other. You don't have to love each other, but try to get along so as not to cause grief to your mother and stepfather. Try to avoid that. As you wrote, they landed on your head. You don't have to love them; just try to allow your mother her happiness without causing aggravation. Try to make her happy. Remember, she was left a widow.

Sibling Rivalry With Special-Needs Siblings

Q *Can Rabbi Bender address the topic of sibling rivalry in families with children who have Down syndrome?*

A We have the great *zechus* in our yeshivah to accept boys with all types of issues. We have a mainstream yeshivah. *Baruch Hashem*, we have boys who become roshei yeshivah, doctors, lawyers, and accountants, and many of them are also noteworthy *talmidei chachamim.*

But we have something else, too. Our students have learned how to live with all kinds of kids. People in our yeshivah believe that we are doing a tremendous *chessed* by helping all types of boys. Correct, absolutely correct! But the greatest *chessed* is to our own *talmidim*! They learn how to be sensitive to other people. A number of our *talmidim* now live in adult homes. Their classmates from twenty years ago, many married with families, still stay in close contact and even visit them regularly. So tell me, who is the *chessed* for?

I have the *zechus* of working with Samcheinu, an organization for widows. I attend their annual Shabbos retreat. I remember that in the very beginning, I met a very young widow who told me that three months prior to her husband passing away, they were blessed with an eighth child, who had Down syndrome. I asked her, "How are you managing?" Her response was, "Are you kidding? This child was the biggest *berachah* for our family. Our kids realized that Mommy cannot do this alone, and they all coalesced around this baby and each became the big brother and sister they needed to become."

We must all realize that Hashem sends these children for a purpose. Our job is to grab the opportunity. I understand it can be very difficult, but these kids are exceptional. Not a bad cell in their bodies, always smiling, always happy, always caring about others. Always worrying about their parents. And always being special. It is up to *Klal Yisrael* to have the right mindset.

Rav Elya Svei *zt"l* used to respond to many questions with, *"Vos vil der Eibishter?"* I think we all know what He wants. For *Klal Yisrael* to do the right thing.

Bottom line, once we realize who these kids are, how could we ever fight with our brothers and sisters? These kids never fight. How can we?

I want to close with a story. In the last few months of her life, just before she went into a coma, I went to spend the night with my mother. My oldest sibling, Rebbetzin Epstein *a"h*, came downstairs to join me. My mother was in a deep sleep, or so we thought. Suddenly, my mother blurted out to my sister, "Esther Mousha, please make sure none of the kids ever fight with each other." I sincerely believe that the six of us were wonderful with each other and never had a real fight or rivalry. Yet my mother, in the last words we remember her saying, admonished us that we should never fight. The worst nightmare of parents is when siblings do not get along.

In these difficult days, let us resolve to have *shalom* in all of *Klal Yisrael*, particularly in our families.

Where Did It Go?

Q In order to get my young children to eat, we sometimes play the following game. I'll give them their food and they'll say, "Tatty, don't look." I'll look away while they eat, and then I will turn around and ask where the food went. They will make up places for me to "look for their food" and I pretend to be annoyed when I don't find it there, until finally they "admit" that they ate it.

My wife and I were wondering if this type of game is perhaps training the kids not to be emesdig. Should we stop playing it?

A This kind of game is perfectly fine. We all do these types of things with our kids. Who hasn't made believe that their spoon or fork was an airplane while feeding their baby? After all is said and done, they know you know they are making things up. They are well aware that it is a game. The most important thing is to always be normal. And this is normal.

Call Me!

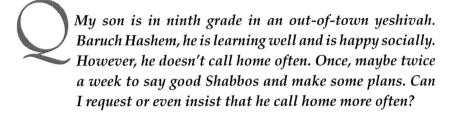

Q *My son is in ninth grade in an out-of-town yeshivah. Baruch Hashem, he is learning well and is happy socially. However, he doesn't call home often. Once, maybe twice a week to say good Shabbos and make some plans. Can I request or even insist that he call home more often?*

A Most kids do not call home often enough. I speak with the *bachurim* all the time in our Mesivta and Beis Medrash on this topic. It is my opinion that a boy should call his mother every day, even if it is only for two minutes, including Erev Shabbos and Motza'ei Shabbos, seven days a week. Why not? I imagine it must depend on what type of home children grow up in. If a child grows up in a home where his/her parents call their parents daily or twice a day, these children will not have to be prompted to call. If the opposite is true, don't expect your children to call you. Like anything else, here even more so, it should be happening by osmosis.

Commuting to a New School

Q *Our family of seven is in the process of moving to a new city. Our children are registered in schools there starting at the beginning of the school year. They range in age from five to twelve. The problem is that renovations on our home extended past the expected date and we will not be able to move in until the beginning of October. Finding a place to rent in our new hometown is difficult and extremely costly.*

Should we commute every day over an hour each way from our current home to our new location so that the children can start school at the beginning of the school year? Or should we enroll them in their former schools for September and then switch them once we have moved?

While I have no wish to put pressure on you, the best thing is for them to commute every day. I personally did this with my own children in 1983 through November. You have accomplished the miracle of getting all your children into good schools in your new location. Don't squander this miracle.

But, then again, if commuting is not a possibility, don't worry. They will switch in October and be just fine.

A Problem of Peyos

My son is fourteen years old. Until recently, he had peyos down to his shoulders. He had always intended to cut them before his bar mitzvah, and Rabbi Bender advised us to compromise and let him cut them to a bit under the ear lobe, which we did.

However, the next day I saw that he had cut them again to the middle of his ear. I told him I was disappointed and unhappy about what he had done. He has also begun to "forget" his hat when he goes away for Shabbos. I am afraid he is slipping.

It is not the end of the world. Stop fighting with him. Kids who have long *peyos* in an environment where most don't will naturally come to resent them, and that will happen when they enter the age of consciousness of their looks — exactly the age your son is now. If you were a chassidish family and you insisted that your son grow very long *peyos*, that would be quite understandable. But when you send your son to a so-called litvishe yeshivah like ours, where almost no one grows very long *peyos* and the parent body is split 50-50 between those who have *peyos* behind their ears and those who don't have *peyos* behind their ears, then you are hurting yourself and the results will be exactly as you are encountering now. Don't let it get to you and don't try to force-feed religion. Your son is not rejecting Torah and mitzvos. Let him find his way.

Don't Fight the Harry Potter Craze

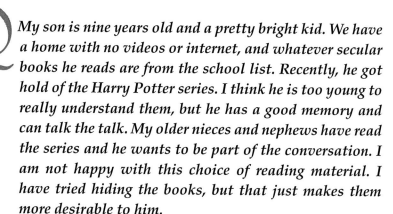

Q *My son is nine years old and a pretty bright kid. We have a home with no videos or internet, and whatever secular books he reads are from the school list. Recently, he got hold of the Harry Potter series. I think he is too young to really understand them, but he has a good memory and can talk the talk. My older nieces and nephews have read the series and he wants to be part of the conversation. I am not happy with this choice of reading material. I have tried hiding the books, but that just makes them more desirable to him.*

Recently, my sister-in-law bought her sons a $100 Harry Potter Lego set. My son begged for one and I told him, "That will not come into our house." But last week, not knowing I had said that, my son's uncle bribed him to do something by promising him a Harry Potter Lego set. My son told me "See, Ma? I davened for the Lego set even though you said it won't come into our house. Hashem can do anything."

Do I allow it in the house after I said I wouldn't? Do I just hope he will play with it for a while and then lose interest? Should I take away the books but let him play with the Lego?

A From your question, it appears to me that you are worrying too much! You have a very good child. No one went off the *derech* from reading Harry Potter books or playing with Harry Potter toys. You have every right and are correct in fighting to keep these books and others like it out of your house. But it should not be World War III. If you make these things into a huge problem, you will create your own monster, and ultimately you will be your own family's worst problem. It may not be ideal, but let it be! It is just a fad that will change dramatically as he gets older in the not too distant future.

Many years ago, before Amazon days, I went to visit a camp in the mountains. As I passed the office, I noticed there were about a hundred boxes from a book distributor. They were all Harry Potter books! I asked the camp director what was going on. He told me that every book has an official publication date. Eighty-four parents ordered the books to be delivered to their sons on the date of publication! I was appalled. How could they spoil their children like this? But then again, is this the worst *aveirah*? Certainly not. Were the parents wrong? Certainly yes. But we must live with the fact that Harry Potter is all over. When we ban too many things, it brings trouble. Let him be! The more of a *tzimmes* you make, the worse it will be.

"Everyone Has One!"

Q My daughter in tenth grade has been asking for a cell phone for at least two years. Of the several dozen girls in her grade, probably nearly every one of them has a cell phone. We have discussed with her the possibility of getting a kosher flip phone with talk text and camera but no web or email capability. Do you think this is reasonable at her age and circumstance?

A This is absolutely fine. (I cannot believe you got away with withholding it until now!) But please make sure that there are indeed almost no children without a phone. Sometimes kids like to say "EVERYONE" has a phone, and then you find out it isn't so.

Supervised Sports App

Q I am wondering about allowing my son going into eleventh grade to have a sports app on his phone (filtered by TAG). This app would allow him to check scores and keep up with his favorite players. My husband feels it will be a distraction, but I feel it is okay if not abused.

A It is never healthy to ban everything. I think you are correct, but he certainly should not have his phone during class time! At night, under parental supervision, but that's it. I give you a *berachah* that his *yetzer hara* shouldn't be worse than this!

Setting Limits on Video Games

Q My oldest son is twelve years old and in seventh grade. Baruch Hashem, we have much nachas from him. He is growing well and is beginning to develop a "Gemara kupp."

However, he frustrates easily and has never taken to any hobbies or sports. There are very few things that interest him, to the point that it is hard to buy him gifts or give him incentives, as so little tickles his fancy.

Reading is one thing he really enjoys. The other is video games. We have always treated video games as something b'dieved. We have allowed it sporadically at Bubby's house or in other limited ways but have never bought such a thing. (Obviously, we make sure the games are innocuous, impose time limits, and provide parental supervision.)

But as he grows older and pressures mount and his downtime becomes more limited, is allowing video games *the proper thing to do? For example, he offered to better memorize shakla vetarya in exchange for a new game. NOTHING else can motivate him to do that. But it would make "gaming" a more permanent fixture in his life.*

Bottom line: With proper hagdaros in place, are video games something like basketball, a healthy outlet, or should they continue to be passively discouraged?

A Your son is a perfectly normal, healthy child, *baruch Hashem*. Technology is a struggle for this entire *dor*. You should allow the games but with strict time limits. Half an hour maximum per night; an hour if you must. He must decide which game(s) he will spend his limited time on. Time limits seem to work best in this kind of situation.

Tracking the iPod

Q *As per your guidance, I bought an iPod Touch for my daughter this week. I have not yet set it up, and she is anxious for me to do so.*

There are apps I can install that record every key stroke and message sent or received. I can then receive regular reports on her activity. I think that if I were to do this, I would have to let her know, both by halachic and legal standards.

Is it advisable to do this, or should I just rely on her knowing that I can and will inspect her device without warning on a regular basis?

A It is definitely advisable to install such an app. You are her father. Nowhere in halachah does it say that a father cannot be a father. Furthermore, I would not rely on inspecting her device. Kids quickly learn to delete their history and cover their tracks.

To Scoot or Not to Scoot

Q I have a question regarding my twelve-year-old son. He is a really good boy, baruch Hashem. He's in a mainstream yeshivah and he wants an electric scooter like many boys have to get to school. Right now he bikes. I'm an old-fashioned type of parent and think that is much better for him.

A Personally, I do not like electric scooters because I think they are unsafe, and I am surprised that they have become so commonplace. That said, as they have become so ubiquitous, if your son is a normal, healthy child, you can buy a non-electric scooter for him.

Chilled About Not Working

Q My fifteen-year-old daughter attended a three-week travel camp. In ten days, she will be going to another sleepaway camp. My wife and I arranged for her to work in a day camp during the interim days so that she would be occupied and not waste ten days and so she would do something productive.

However, my daughter does not want to work. She does not know anyone else working in this camp and did not understand that we were arranging this for her. She says she just wants to "chill" for a few days between the two trips. We have tried offering rewards, but she still refuses. She is not a hard-working or ambitious child in general, as my other children are, and we had hoped this would teach her some responsibility.

A   When it comes to children, you have to pick your battles. This is especially true with fifteen-year-olds. It is perfectly normal for a kid returning from a long trip to want to "chill" for ten days. I would not make a big deal over this. Let her chill out and relax. She might not be as academic as your other children, but teenage girls live under stress the entire school year. They worry about their school marks much more than the boys. Let her be. As a suggestion: Fathers are very important for girls this age. Take her out to eat twice over the ten-day period. Bond with her and tell her that you love her so she will not worry that you are disappointed in her for not working.

Video Games for Long Winter Nights

Q   *What is Rabbi Bender's opinion on electronic games without internet access? On long winter nights, there is not much for my twelve-year-old son to do, and though we don't have any electronic devices yet, I was considering one.*

A   If all the other kids have video games, and he is asking for it, you must get him something. Just be careful with what you get him, and make time limits daily. Remember that if you won't help him, at least a little bit, he will get it elsewhere. And then you will have no control over what he is seeing.

Masmid in Training

Q   *During Covid, our bar mitzvah-aged son became a world-class masmid. He started to follow daf yomi, but we don't know how much he really understands. He continues to make sure to attend daf yomi even though school* and camp have resumed. He is also trying to finish *Shishah Sidrei Mishnah for his bar mitzvah. In general, he is a well-adjusted kid who is happy-go-lucky and has many friends. But we are worried he may burn out. Should we try to stop him from his extra learning?*

A There are sometimes wonderful, normal children who are also able to spend hours a day learning. Keep a very close eye on him, but do not hold him back from any of this. *Iy"H* he will turn out to be a real *gadol b'Yisrael*.

Keep the Geshmak

Q *My thirteen-year-old son is having a great year in yeshivah, baruch Hashem. However, while he comprehends concepts and is able to be medameh milta l'milta and does well on tests, he is not doing well with reading and translating. I asked him to prepare just one line of Gemara, and he is very resistant. I am wondering if the Aramaic along with all the new concepts is just too overwhelming for him.*

My instinct is to stop nudging him about the reading and just focus on the Gemara outside. I figure he can always catch up with the reading down the road, and the geshmak of a svara and shakla vetarya is presently more important to nurture. Does that make sense?

A You are absolutely correct. Keep the *geshmak*, and certainly don't do anything to turn him off from learning. *Iy"H*, one day it will all fall into place.

Money Matters

Tuition Break
Does Not Change Need for Camp

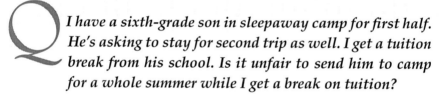

Q *I have a sixth-grade son in sleepaway camp for first half. He's asking to stay for second trip as well. I get a tuition break from his school. Is it unfair to send him to camp for a whole summer while I get a break on tuition?*

A Camp in today's age is an absolute necessity. It is fine to do this.

Paying for Treats

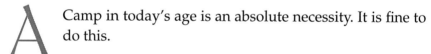

Q *We have two daughters aged 12 and 14. Now that they are teenagers, they frequently ask to go out with friends for ice cream, pizza, Slurpees, etc.*

I was wondering what Rabbi Bender's thoughts are on encouraging the girls to pay for most of these trips with their own money. We are okay with paying once in a while, but feel that they should learn the value of money by using their own earned money to pay for "extras" such as these. Especially when they request it so often. (Aside from the fact that we are not financially well off.)

A You are correct. Children should learn responsibility and the value of money. Have them pay every other time.

By the way, please don't wear the fact that you are not financially well off on your sleeves. Kids don't want to be known as a shleppy poor family. Being not well off should not be a consideration when making a decision like your question about ice cream.

Our family was not well-off financially after my father passed away, but my mother never allowed us to think like that. Somehow, she managed fine and always gave us what we needed. She kept up the *simchas hachaim* in our family, and we never felt the pain of not having. You don't want this to be a pressure on your children.

Weekly Allowance
Is Not Payment for Chores

Q *What is Rabbi Bender's opinion on the following? We have two small children, ages seven and five. We'd like to give them some small change for extra jobs they do (over and above their regular responsibilities); for example, if they help out extra on Erev Shabbos or help clean up the playroom. We thought it would be a nice way to put some small change in their piggy banks. Is this the right chinuch approach? Will it train them to want money for anything they do to help?*

A I never liked this practice. Kids should automatically have short, small tasks. Training them to get money for that is not a good idea. There's nothing wrong with a weekly allowance, but don't tie it to chores.

Sharing the Paycheck

Q I just got a really well-paying job, and my married brother keeps telling me I should give my mother a portion of my money. I want to keep the money I earn, but I feel so selfish.

A If your mother is struggling after working hard to make ends meet, then your brother is correct. That is only if you are able to spare some of your salary. If you are putting some in savings, divide the savings portion. It is important to save, but also to help your parent. Years ago, it was standard for working children to hand over their entire wages to their parents. Things are different now, but it is still proper to help your mother in this way.

Investment in Tznius Will Pay Off

Q My eldest daughter is almost fifteen and in the ninth grade. She went to a Modern Orthodox elementary school where I placed her before we became more frum. We chose a high school for her that is also more on the modern side and has girls that are not necessarily from religious backgrounds, but has the right hashkafos and is known to be very loving and produce girls who have good middos and grow religiously, usually becoming fully frum. We felt this would be a good place for her and not too much of a culture shock compared to a typical Bais Yaakov.

The issue is a conversation she and I had regarding tznius. She feels that it is very hard for her to wear skirts because she looks better in pants. (She also mentioned that she is one of the few girls in her class who wear *skirts.) We had a conversation about halachah, and that my role as a parent is to teach her what is correct and what is not and to set standards for the household. Ultimately, her relationship with Hashem is hers, and if she finds this is an area that is difficult for her, then that is something to focus on and try to grow in. Of course, I emphasized that I love her regardless and what she does as an adult is between her and Hashem.*

She then mentioned that she might feel better about wearing skirts if she felt better about her appearance overall — if she got her hair straightened and took care of her skin, nails, and other beauty regimens that women typically engage in. I thought this was a great idea. I was encouraged by the fact that her issue with tznius seems to be a confidence issue and not a hashkafic one. I am happy to pay for these extras and see it as my role as her mother and an investment in her overall spirituality.

However, my husband disagrees and sees this as frivolous. He doesn't see why she needs to focus on making herself look prettier as she is not dating, etc. He said he is willing to compromise and pay half of these expenses if she pays the other half from her babysitting money. He believes strongly in the children being financially responsible and learning to earn money and pay for extras.

I agree with this stance in general. She is a responsible girl who pays for other expenses for herself regularly. My husband's idea is a compromise, but I still feel strongly that this is something we should fund fully, and that it's our responsibility as her parents, especially in light of her tznius issue.

 You are correct. You should pay fully. There are few things more important to an adolescent or teenaged girl than her appearance. By funding these things, you will enable her to dress in a more *tzniusdig* fashion while maintaining her self-esteem, thus removing added pressure. As she gains more and more confidence, you will see the dividends, *b'ezras Hashem.*

~

Choices, Choices — Selecting the Right School for Your Child

Sending Brothers to the Same Yeshivah

Q I have an eighth-grade son and we are applying to mesivtos now. I have a son in ninth grade in a yeshivah near
our home, and that's where my eighth grader's rebbis
and principals feel he should go. It is the only mesivta he
wants to go to, but I know it's not such a good idea to
send brothers to the same yeshivah if they are only one
grade apart.

A There is nothing wrong with sending two brothers to the
same mesivta, unless one is way, way ahead of the other
academically or socially. It really depends on circumstances. If there is no great jealousy between the two of them, and
you are happy with the first mesivta, send your next one there.
There are certain *mosdos* that don't want to accept brothers who
are close in age. That is fine. But for you, why not? I know one
family that has six boys in six different *mosdos*. I don't get it! Do
they *davka* want to attend six dinners a year?

Keep Him in Playgroup One More Year

Q Before the start of the school year, I hesitated as to whether to hold my four-year-old son back in school. But the playgroup where I was considering sending him (to give him another year of playgroup before kindergarten) filled up, so I ended up putting him into kindergarten. Recently, my son mentioned that some children in his class were saying not nice things to him. At first, when we asked about it, he said that even with that, he liked school. Then, yesterday, he did not want to go to school in the morning, though it's not clear that that is why.

Because of this and my previous concerns, I am wondering if the fact that we're already seeing small issues now (he is not super put-together) means that he will struggle in school for years to come. I wonder if many issues would resolve themselves if he were just held back a year, giving him an extra year before kindergarten. Meanwhile, spots have opened up in the playgroup I had been considering. Should I pull him out and put him in the playgroup and try kindergarten again next year? The issues are not big, but they are there.

A No question about it. Put him back in playgroup now. There is no reason to gamble with your son. It is always best to play it safe in a situation like this. When there is a chance to help a young child by holding him/her back, then of course, do so! The only time, perhaps, not to leave a child back is when the child, for example, has very weak comprehension. Holding him back will do very little for him. In such an instance it is not a mitzvah to hold the student back.

Repeating Pre-1A

Q My son is supposed to be entering first grade next year. He is the youngest boy in the class, but very bright. However, he struggles socially. He deals with a certain amount of stress because I am divorced and there are things about his father that confuse him that I can't really explain to him. My instinct was to hold him back a year, but I am afraid he will be very bored academically. My experience with my other children is that sitting bored in class was torture for them. However, socially, I am sure he would be happier if he was left back. What is the right thing to do?

A I don't think there is any question. You must leave him back. Make him feel like he is somebody important, with any idea you can think of. For example, say that the rebbi needs an assistant and he loves you so much, he wants you to be his helper. It always pays to err on the side of caution in these types of situations. Letting him go to first grade is a gamble, and you should never gamble with your children. The fact that you are divorced has absolutely no bearing on the situation. These cases are almost always open-and-shut situations. Do the right thing and you will see *siyata diShmaya*!

No Pushing!

Q We have a son who will be turning four at the beginning of the school year. We aren't sure if we should start him in school next year or the year after. His playgroup morah says he is doing really well and is average among his classmates. She doesn't think he needs to be held back, but agreed he might be better off with older *three-year-olds next year than with four-year-olds. In addition, my son is on the quiet side and small in stature.*

A Keep him back. Especially because he is short, there is no question about it. In ninety-five percent of these cases, it is better to keep the child back. Period! No ifs, ands, or buts! And don't let your husband push you in the other direction. Fathers are anxious to see their brilliant son already in Lakewood or Brisk. Or Harvard for that matter. Mothers have the intuition, foresight, patience, and *binah yeseirah* to take things one day at a time.

There is an exception to the rule about keeping back. If a child is weak academically and is socially fine, I don't know if it is a mitzvah to keep the child back. You will gain very little. Keeping him back will *lav davka* help him improve academically. He is weak and it will take as many as fifteen years to get him on track. In such a case, let him at least be comfortable with his environs, enjoy friends his age, etc.

Another Year of Kindergarten Is Best

Q *Our daughter has just finished kindergarten and it was recommended that she repeat the grade. The morah is not confident with her knowledge of the aleph-beis, and she still has trouble when assigned a classroom activity or instruction. The principal feels very strongly that she needs to repeat. However, she has many friends and plays very nicely with the other girls in the class. She comes across as an intelligent child and does not seem delayed or special needs in any way.*

We are not sure that holding her back will help. She may struggle anyway. Will it embarrass her to be the oldest child in the class, repeating a grade, and still be academically behind? Or will she do better staying with the appropriate age group and possibly needing extra help (as many students do because this is a very high-level school)?

A This is a question that arises again and again. In nearly every case, I advise keeping the child back. My wife insisted that it would be best if some of our children and grandchildren repeated a grade, and I am always grateful for those decisions. If you move her ahead, and she has to repeat a grade later in life, it will be MUCH harder for her. The bottom line is, if you send her ahead you are gambling. If you have her repeat, you are giving her the chance of a smoother ride through elementary and eventually high school. This is exactly what my wife and I would do.

Repeat the Year to Pick Up the Basics

Q *Our son just completed Pre-1A and we are unsure whether we should promote him to first grade or have him repeat Pre-1A. He is a smart boy in general, with good havanah in areas like parashah, Yamim Tovim, etc. He is very on the ball socially as well. However, he has a hard time with basic skills like numbers, letters, name recall, berachos recall, etc. He did manage to pick up kriah very well through one-on-one tutoring. Though his weakness in these areas made it hard for him to follow in class when it came to technical, skill-based work, we are noticing that as of now, his auditory system seems to be picking up, and he is remembering words of berachos and songs more accurately.*

As the year progressed, his behavior in class deteriorated. Some of his teachers felt that due to his perfectionistic and emotionally sensitive nature, he sensed his weaknesses and acted out as a result. We have seen this at home as well. For example, if he is not doing well in a game, he will mess up the whole game and storm away. We have had to pick him up from school several times when he became uncooperative and aggressive.

Because of all these things, maybe it would make sense to hold him back. This way he will feel more on top of the game academically, and will hopefully be more at ease and more cooperative.

On the other hand, we are concerned that he will feel so badly about being held back that he will have an even harder time functioning in the classroom. He may also be bored during kriah instruction, which can cause a behavior problem.

A This is easy. There is nothing to talk about. He needs to mature. Even leaving him back, some issues may continue for a bit. With children like this, always play it safe. Keep him back now, while he is still young. Don't worry about his feeling bad. Bribe him if you have to. But he should repeat. *Hatzlachah*! And I don't really know of a single case where a four- or 5-year-old that was left back has had negative ramifications in the future. Maybe for two days, but that's it!

No Pressure, Please

Q *I work in a reputable school in my neighborhood. The school is known to be professional, well run, and warm. The Hebrew principal is especially known to instill the girls with strong hashkafos and a love for Torah and mitzvos.*

I have two concerns, though. The school places a very strong emphasis on academics and is known to be a hard school. My child's birthday is at the end of October, and she will be young for the grade. Although I have no reason to suspect she will have learning issues, I have no reason to believe she will be above average either. I am concerned about placing her in such an intense academic environment.

My second concern is that the Hebrew principal hires extremely young teachers straight out of seminary. The principal demands a lot of her teachers in terms of covering a certain amount of material. Parents have complained that the teachers are very young and pressured to please the principal and finish the curriculum. This does not allow them time to focus on anything aside from covering ground. Parents have complained that if anything comes up, these young teachers are too inexperienced or are too busy focusing on the curriculum to deal with anything.

The other school I am considering, also a very reputable school, is well run, but possibly not as professional. It is known to be extremely warm and not as academic. I'm getting mixed reports, but some people feel that the academics may be less than average. However, this school looks to hire experienced teachers, and the principal and staff are known to be extremely involved in helping with anything that may come up.

Considering that I work in the first school, is there enough of a reason to consider the second?

A Your letter is rather lengthy; I am sorry that my response will be very short!

There is no question you should choose the second school. Unnecessary pressure is not beneficial for a child. There is no reason to put pressure on your daughter, even if she is a good student.

Keeping Him Back Will Not Be Beneficial

Q I live in an out-of-town city where there is not a big choice of schools. All my children attended the same school, where my youngest is entering grade 1. He has some learning/processing issues and will need extra help. Socially, he is terrific and on the ball, very popular, a good ballplayer, tall, and a leader. The school wants him to repeat Pre-1A. He was born in March, but their cut-off is September 1, which means he will be a year to a year and a half older than other boys in Pre-1A. What should we do?

A Normally, I am a proponent of having a child repeat a grade, and at the earliest age possible. However, in this case, I do not see anything to gain. The child is socially adept and "with it"; putting him back will hurt him badly. He is going to need long-term intervention, which will not be solved by keeping him back this year. Most of the time, a child will be kept back because he is immature, young, and needs to develop. Keeping such a child back makes sense. But in your case, it would be self-defeating.

Do whatever you can to have his tutoring done in school, not at home when he should be playing.

Hatzlachah.

Too Many Switches Can Be Detrimental to the Children

Q Until recently, I was Rosh Kollel in a Sephardic kollel in our neighborhood. At the time, a new Sephardic school opened, run in part by my then-employer. Under pressure *from my employer, we switched our two youngest boys to this new school. The older of the two spent his last two years of preschool there. Baruch Hashem, he had a great rebbi in Pre-1A and learned to read beautifully with a true Sephardic havarah.*

During that year, my position changed, and I am no longer the Rosh Kollel of that kollel. We moved from the area and switched my boys back to the Ashkenazi yeshivah in which they had been enrolled originally. The older of these two sons just completed first grade. He did struggle for a few months with the change of havarah, but overall he transitioned well.

I was now offered a shteller in yet another mossad which is more of a heimishe yeshivah. They use a chassidishe havarah and teitch in Yiddish. With this new shteller, I am being asked to switch my two boys to this third mossad. I'm comfortable with the mossad. My younger son is only four and I have no issue switching him.

The question is regarding my seven-year-old. If we switch him this fall for second grade, it will be three different schools in three years, all with different havaros. Is this detrimental for him? Our biggest concern is his feeling of stability, with so many changes in a relatively short time and his davening and kriah skills not yet fully developed. It has been made clear by my employer that the switch is expected unless it will damage the child.

A I would not switch either boy. If you switch them again, you may in all likelihood damage both children, shattering their sense of stability, as you predicted. Don't you dare do it! You are gambling with the sanity of your children.

Dealing With Behavioral Challenges

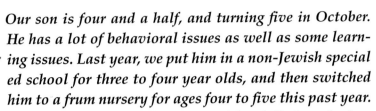 Our son is four and a half, and turning five in October. He has a lot of behavioral issues as well as some learning issues. Last year, we put him in a non-Jewish special ed school for three to four year olds, and then switched him to a frum nursery for ages four to five this past year.

He is currently in day camp with a full-time shadow and other additional help. He has been manifesting serious issues and is currently on meds by his treating psychiatrist, who believes his behavior may be symptomatic of OCD.

Our options for the coming school year are as follows:

1. Continue in his current school into kindergarten and pursue the pendency process, which would give him ten hours of SEIT and some ABA hours. I would likely need to find the para providers, which is very difficult, and switch my insurance to cover the para, which would increase my expenses.

2. Switch my son over to the special ed school for behaviorally challenged kids, where our older son is and doing very well.

His day camp did not allow him to join without a full-time para, so a para will definitely be needed if he continues in his current school.

Should we try to mainstream our son now and keep him in his current school where they will work with us, keeping in mind that the burden of taking care of his services will basically fall on me? Or should we switch him to the special ed school and hope that as he gets older he will be able to be mainstreamed?

A Keep him in his current school. That is your best bet. Let him have ten hours of SEIT in a regular school. Let him be as normal as possible. If you see that after sincere effort it is not working out, switch him to the special ed school.

In general, I am not sure you should be accepting so many ideas based on your experience with your older son. While these things may indeed be genetic, we should not be assigning your son to special ed and all kinds of meds at such a young age. Getting some good educators involved in your son's *chinuch* is the way to go. First, try to have him be "normal." If after a few years it is not a go, we will worry about it then.

No Reason to Change Schools

Q *I have been teaching in a Modern Orthodox school in Brooklyn since my children's father and I divorced. My children attend this school. They are comfortable and happy there. I have since remarried.*

However, in the past several years, I have moved to the right hashkafically. I am considering switching my younger child to a school that is more in line with my hashkafos. She is bubbly and fun and makes friends easily. She also generally rolls with the punches. However, I wonder if this is the right move, as there has been a lot of change in her life, between the divorce and my new husband, and school is a stable thing in her life. In addition, she has ADHD and has a team in place in the school she is currently in that has worked hard to get her to where she is academically and emotionally.

A There is no question in my mind that you should not move your child. Even without the ADHD piece, if she is comfortable and happy, I wouldn't move her. Considering that the current school is working successfully with her ADHD issues, there is certainly no question.

Choices, Choices — Selecting the Right School for Your Child

Make the Switch

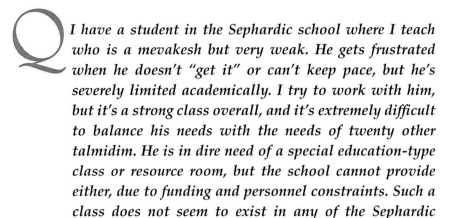 *I have a student in the Sephardic school where I teach who is a mevakesh but very weak. He gets frustrated when he doesn't "get it" or can't keep pace, but he's severely limited academically. I try to work with him, but it's a strong class overall, and it's extremely difficult to balance his needs with the needs of twenty other talmidim. He is in dire need of a special education-type class or resource room, but the school cannot provide either, due to funding and personnel constraints. Such a class does not seem to exist in any of the Sephardic schools in our area.*

His parents are turning to me for advice. It comes down to a question of his staying in his current surroundings, which enables him to learn with the Sephardic havarah and to learn the halachos in a way that is geared to his upbringing, and be with kids from his community, or to move him to an Ashkenazi school that has the learning support system he needs to grow. What should be done?

I have said it before and I will restate it. After a healthy, happy home, success in school is the most important factor in a child's wellbeing. There is no question he should attend a program that will suit his academic needs, even if it is Ashkenazi. His academic future and more depend on it.

Non-Jewish Special Ed School
Is Mandatory

Q My two-and-a-half-year-old son has been receiving speech and special-instruction therapies. He is a very bright kid, but has some developmental delays and behavioral issues. He was given a diagnosis of autism two months ago.

He has been approved for a special education placement for ages three to five. He is also approved for speech, physical therapy, and occupational therapy.

We now have two options:

1) To send him to a special ed preschool where he would get all the therapies he needs in a small setting. But it is not a Jewish school. He would be in a class of twelve with three teachers. (They are very accommodating regarding kashrus, etc.)

2) To decline his special ed placement and put him in a regular preschool where he would be with frum kids. He would still be pulled out for his therapies, but that would be a larger class with only one teacher.

Do I put him in the non-Jewish school so he can have the smaller class setting, or do I put him in a Jewish school where he may not be getting as much help?

A There is no question you should give him the best education possible for the next few years. Sure, it would be nice to have him in a mainstream yeshivah, but at this age the risk with public school is finite. I know of many such cases. In the long term, it will work out. At this age, you don't need to give the child any extra tutoring in *limudei kodesh* as your own *chinuch* will be sufficient. *Iy"H*, you will see much *nachas* from him.

Sometimes Public School
Is a Temporary Answer

Q I live out of town and have an eight-year-old daughter with severe dyslexia. Though it breaks my heart, it appears I have to put her in public school, as our school here is not equipped to handle her issues. Am I doing the right thing? I have exhausted all other options. Should we consider moving our family to the East Coast? How can I ensure that she stays on the right derech?

A Not all kids on the East Coast are in yeshivah either. There are dyslexic children here who are in public school too. What we do in our yeshivah is that whenever the public schools are off, such as for their holidays, etc., we allow the public school children to come to our yeshivah. They can join a class of children their age, make friends, and stay within the social circle of the yeshivah. So for the time being, keep a close eye on her in public school. If you notice she is picking up the wrong things, then remove her. It would also be very helpful if you get her a mentor/*chavrusa* who comes to the house twice a week or so and helps her keep up to some extent with *limudei kodesh.* This can be a high school girl. She should be *geshmak* and personable. Such an arrangement can make a world of difference.

I was recently visited by a couple from out of town. Their dilemma was that their twelve-year-old daughter, very academically handicapped, is still in the public school system, going into seventh grade. I was incredulous! How can we send a twelve year old girl into a public school? The chances of her being abused are very great! There is only one school in the town. The other children of this couple attend that school.

I immediately picked up the phone and called the *menahel* with whom I am somewhat acquainted. I asked how they are allowing something like this. The family can't move for many reasons. The girl is not a troublemaker. Just super *shvach*. I insisted that they find a way to have the girl as part of a regular class and be pulled out as much as humanly possible without turning the kid into more of a basket case. And if she doesn't get the greatest report cards, who cares! We have to save this *neshamah*! Who created this girl as handicapped — the *Ribbono Shel Olam*! It is a *nisayon*, not only for the immediate family but for every single person in that city. The rest of the classmates are not stupid. Make the girl a *chessed* project without her knowing about it.

Incidentally, as I write this, I don't know what ultimately happened for this school year.

Unfortunately, this goes on much too much. It is our job as *mechanchim* to take care of every single *neshamah* in our *mossad* or neighborhood!

Special Ed vs. Mainstreaming

Q Our son has spent the past year in a special education setting. He is not ready to mainstream. His rebbi feels that without the extra help that he receives there, he will be lost in class. The special education supervisor feels the same.

The program he attends has the same rebbi this year, which is wonderful. He is phenomenal and really gets our son. However, this program moves from school to school each year, and this year it is in a school that has vastly different hashkafos from ours. We can see that this is affecting our son. What is more important at this point? To focus on academics and leave him where he is, or to put him in a regular classroom in a school where the social and hashkafic elements are vastly preferable?

A It strongly depends on two things: the age of the child, and how far behind he is. Up until the age of ten or eleven, the longer you give the child educational support, the better it will be in the long run. The fact that he is in an environment not conducive to your *hashkafah* can be overcome. When children are at this age, their lives revolve around school. If they are not successful in school, it affects their entire being — and their future. Therefore, focus on academics first. Remember that next year he will again be in a different setting. This arrangement is not permanent. *Im yirtzeh Hashem*, he will be fine.

But if the child is already twelve or thirteen, he has most likely begun to develop, and the sooner you can get him back into an environment more to your liking the better, unless the child is significantly handicapped. It seems from your question that the *matzav* is not that bad. You will need to talk it over with someone you trust educationally.

Save Your Child With Special Ed Program

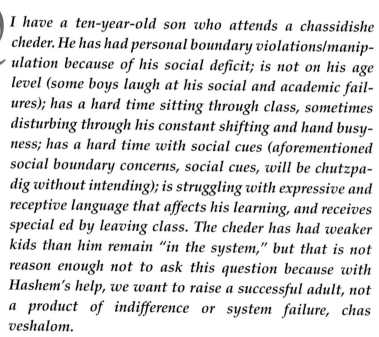 *I have a ten-year-old son who attends a chassidishe cheder. He has had personal boundary violations/manipulation because of his social deficit; is not on his age level (some boys laugh at his social and academic failures); has a hard time sitting through class, sometimes disturbing through his constant shifting and hand busyness; has a hard time with social cues (aforementioned social boundary concerns, social cues, will be chutzpadig without intending); is struggling with expressive and receptive language that affects his learning, and receives special ed by leaving class. The cheder has had weaker kids than him remain "in the system," but that is not reason enough not to ask this question because with Hashem's help, we want to raise a successful adult, not a product of indifference or system failure, chas veshalom.*

This question is being asked with "belonging" in

mind because of potential at-risk concerns (he is a sensory-seeker and risk-taker; has sneaked a little alcohol at a kiddush; has a hard time with "no" and tries to get his way relentlessly; has difficulty with social cues; is enamored with what is considered "cool style" dressing by the fringe in our community). Is it better to switch him to a different school that is not chassidish where he will feel good about his learning but be in a different school than everyone he knows, or should we keep him in the community cheder where he will be struggling academically (the system highlights his deficits), which may lead him to feel "different" anyway?

Basically, for a ten-year-old chassidishe boy, is it better to "belong" by remaining in the kehillah system (though he might fail in academics or be one of the weaker ones), going out for remedial help, and being a little "less than" in maturity and socially,

Or:

Is it better to send him to a special education class within a small, mainstream, non-kehillah cheder where the learning would be on his academic level and he could succeed academically and socially?

A   There is no question that for a year or two he must go to a special program. Nothing detrimental will happen before he is twelve years old. This is a common question, because unfortunately our own yeshivos do not have adequate programming for such students. I even advise parents to send their children to public school special programs, and here you are asking about a program in a yeshivah that is not to your *heimishe* liking! What you must understand is that your son may be crippled forever; this special program gives you a real chance to help him. Obviously, he has many issues. You must try to solve them! He will be with *Yiddishe kinder* even if they are slightly different from what he is used to. Send him there. Save your child!

Seek Private Help for Reading Disability

Q Our twelve-year-old son has severe reading disabilities. We would like to send him to a special school next year, which will help him greatly. However, he is resistant. He complains that it would completely change his life, he will lose all his friends, and he is not the only one in the class who can't read. He also says if we force him to go, he will not cooperate and will not try to learn to read anyway. What should we do?

A You should never force a child to go anywhere. Certainly, in this case, it would be counterproductive. You will have to get someone to work with him privately. Even if he has to miss school sometimes to enable this, that is what you should do.

Finding the Right Yeshivah for a Twenty-Year-Old Serious Learner

Q Our son is almost twenty. He is a very mature and responsible bachur. He loves to learn and spends most of his free time learning in shul. However, he has a hard time with the pace in most yeshivos. We found out that he likes to learn quickly. Any shiur is too slow and deep and he has no interest in working on it. He also has a hard time finding a chavrusa who learns at his speed. Last year he had a good night seder chavrusa and was able to finish Masechta Berachos.

We are at a loss as to what he should do now. He doesn't want to go to a yeshivah where he will have to go to shiur, and he's also concerned that he won't be *able to find a chavrusa who will learn at his pace. As of now he has no yeshivah to go to. Do you have any recommendations?*

A There are all types of *bachurim* out there who need all types of learning. Until the end of high school, we try to get everyone on track to be like most others their age. But post-high school, I would say to let them go their own *derech*. Let your son learn to his strengths. There are all kinds of yeshivos today that cater to all kinds of kids. Call me in yeshivah for some suggestions.

Who Will Help Him If Not You?

Q *We had a talmid in our yeshivah two years ago who unfortunately was not doing well, both academically and behaviorally. He has a strong learning disability. Due to the fact that our yeshivah was not equipped to help him, we were considering asking him to leave, but his parents preempted us by pulling him out and putting him in a special program.*

In the middle of this year, the parents approached me and asked me to take this young man back into yeshivah. They have said they will give him whatever he needs to be matzliach and are being very persistent.

To complicate matters, five months ago, the yeshivah went through a transformation, installing a new board of directors. We need to raise the bar and change the name of the yeshivah in order to increase enrollment, which had been falling in the past several years. By accepting this talmid, we will give other parents the feeling that the yeshivah is the same as it was and accepts everyone, no matter how weak.

A If the boy were currently enrolled in your yeshivah, I would say you cannot send him away. But since the parents took him out voluntarily, you do not have to accept him now.

However, it is about time that all schools find a way to educate every single boy who is accepted into their yeshivah! It could very well be that if your yeshivah had had a program for this young man, things would be looking better for him. Now the issue is overwhelming. Must you take the child back, no. Should you try to help him, a resounding yes!

This problem of certain children not getting accepted, particularly into high school and even elementary school, is a terrible one! Just terrible. In your case, you are asking if you must accept him into your school. That is *"ah halber tzarah."* But for schools not to find room in their high schools for every single *neshamah* in their own school is absolutely criminal!

Please notice who are the children who generally don't get in. Most of them, though not always, are children from dysfunctional homes or one-parent homes. If a school is going to reject one of their own, then it is incumbent upon them to ensure that the school gets the child into another school. Merely giving the parents or the child a list of where to apply is a joke! Why should any school accept this child when their old school refuses him?

Rav Pam *zt"l* and *yblct"a* Rav Matisyahu Salomon, together with a very distinguished *askan*, Reb Yisroel Lefkowitz *z"l*, used to make sure that every child gets into a yeshivah! Aren't we doing Hashem's work? Isn't that what we tell people when we go fundraising? Well, Hashem would never abandon any child, no matter how problematic the home is or how difficult the child is. This topic really aches me.

And we get dumped on in our mesivta. Unfairly! We certainly cannot take in every single problematic child. Schools must take care of their own!

Developing Daveners

Underlying Issues Affect Davening

Q My fifteen-year-old son has been diagnosed with numerous issues, from auditory processing disorder to ADD to
ASD. Davening is one of the many things he struggles
with. I would appreciate any eitzos for how to help him
with the upcoming Yamim Tovim. In the past, he has
either come late to shul or not come at all. Most
Shabbosos he doesn't go to shul for Shacharis, either
with his father or by himself. Interestingly, this summer
he went to sleepaway camp for the first time, and he did
enjoy the davening there. He does fairly well in yeshivah. He has a wonderful rebbi whom I am in touch with
daily.

A Your problem is not unusual. Most of the time, at bar
mitzvah, boys with this problem turn around. In that
way, your son is a bit different. I don't know the dynamics of your family, but it seems to me that your husband is not

involved with him enough. He must learn to bond with his son. What I am hearing is that you are doing the worrying, you are the one in touch with the rebbi, etc. This is unusual with a fifteen-year-old. *Baruch Hashem*, yours is not a single-parent home. Your husband must take out your son at least once a month, one on one. He must tell him how important it is for him to daven with his father. If your son cannot sit the entire davening, make some compromises. A teenaged boy needs his father involved every step of the way.

Don't Push and It Will Come

Q*My son is sixteen years old, currently in eleventh grade. Baruch Hashem, he is a healthy and well-functioning teenager for the most part. However, for several years, he has struggled with an inability to wake up in time for yeshivah davening. We have tried incentives and consequences, with little success.*

Baruch Hashem, this past year he has developed quite a love for his learning. He is dorming in his yeshivah, but the problem with waking for Shacharis persists. His rebbi has insisted that something must be done. He suggested that my husband pick him up any day that he misses Shacharis and take him home until the next day. We thought this would be a powerful incentive for my son, but if it is working, it is barely noticeable.

AThis is the biggest problem we have with teenagers who do not have a *geshmak* in davening. Even after they develop the *geshmak*, they find it hard to wake up on time. My feeling is, you should NOT force him to attend yeshivah davening. Let him daven when and where he will, so long as he gets to *shiur* on time. Eventually, once his love for learning is more developed, he will want to be part of davening too.

In fact, I am not sure why his rebbi is so insistent that you must do something about it. What the rebbi is proposing to do is real *halbanas panim* to an otherwise good boy who loves his learning and is just a typical teenager who can't get out of bed in the morning!

Slow down, please, and think of the ramifications to a boy who can develop into a real *ben Torah* once he gets past his immaturity about davening.

Attending Minyan But Not Davening

Q *My son is currently in sixth grade. His rebbi has advised me that, for some time now, my son does not daven when attending minyan in school. He just sits quietly. However, when I take him to shul with me, he does daven certain parts. Yet he insists that he wants to go to minyan in school. Should we allow him to go to the school minyan even though he doesn't participate? Or would it be better to take him to shul with me?*

A What you are describing is perfectly normal for a child of his age. Don't push him. Don't bother him. He will start davening in yeshivah when he feels like it. It can take a very long time. Never force-feed religious issues to children. You may incentivize, but don't be too pushy, as it can backfire.

My Son Doesn't Daven Much

Q *My eighth-grade son comes with me to shul often. I have noticed recently that he just sits there, not saying much of davening. He used to be more "into it." I know davening is a challenge for many English-speaking kids as they don't understand much of what they are saying. Should I do something about this, or just wait it out?*

A You can start an incentive program with him. That can work like magic. Even though he is an eighth-grader, I would not force him to sit through the entire davening. For example, let him stay for *leining* until *shlishi*, then go out for the rest. Don't press him too hard. He clearly has no *cheishek* for *tefillah*. This is not an unusual thing, and you don't want him to completely hate coming to shul. Eventually, he will come around. Incidentally, davening is not necessarily a challenge for American boys because of their unfamiliarity with the words. We are living in a very fast-paced world with excitement and technology all over the place, and suddenly you are asking a boy to sit for a long while.

Rebbeim are known to say these days that they can no longer just teach, they need to entertain, because children are used to ever more stimulating excitement. It is not an easy situation, and it is reflected in children's difficulty with davening, as well.

Going to Minyan on Shabbos

Q *I am wondering how much to push my eleven-year-old to go to minyan on Shabbos? My husband davens hashka-mah on Shabbos because this is what works for his schedule. After Shacharis, he learns and then visits a nursing home. Understandably, my son doesn't want to get up that early. There is a later minyan, and there is almost always an older brother of his in attendance, so it's not like he would have to go alone. Still, he often doesn't go. That is true of Minchah and on Friday nights as well.*

A First of all, your husband should stop davening at the *hashkamah minyan*. He should go to the later *minyan* with his son. That must be his priority. Your son doesn't even have to go on time. He can go a bit later. Also, create incentives and the boy will want to come. And don't force him to sit through the entire davening or more than a portion of the *leining*. After *kiddush* in shul, your son should accompany his father to the nursing home. Then start your *seudah* a bit later.

While some kids still won't daven with a *minyan* even later on, I guarantee that after six months of this he will go to *minyan* of his own volition. Though I am not a *posek*, I believe this is the answer.

Longing to Daven

Q *From the time I was a young girl, my mother pushed me to daven. It was more like I must, and I felt that it was shoved down my throat. I'm a girl who is connected to Hashem and I talk to Him all the time in my own words. But I dream of the day when I'll want to daven and have a cheishek to take out a siddur. There's so much to daven for; sometimes I feel like my life is out of control and I know only Hashem can help me, but I just can't open that siddur. I'm embarrassed and sad to say I have an automatic aversion to davening. What can I do?*

A One of the biggest mistakes some parents make is force-feeding religious issues on their children. They mean well, but children don't take too kindly to it. What is happening to you is exactly the result. Once you realize that davening should not be a burden, but rather a way of connecting, you will start opening the siddur on your own. I suggest you start with five minutes at home. When you are ready, move it up to more. Do not push yourself; let it happen naturally.

Grade Behavior, Not Davening

Q *We are trying to work on davening in our school with a goal of accomplishing the following:*

    1. Increase the talmidim's sense of davening as a responsibility — whether they "feel it" or not.

    2. Motivate them to find meaning in davening

    3. Improve the decorum during davening.

We plan to accomplish this by:

    1. Focusing on the hashkafah of tefillah in class

    2. Dedication class time to teach the meanings of the tefillos

    3. Focusing on reading parts of davening

    4. Giving students a grade on the report card where 60% reflects how much he is davening and 40% reflects behavior during davening.

Our question is about point 4. Do you think, from a hashkafic and chinuch perspective, that it is a good idea to give talmidim a grade on their davening?

A Honestly, I don't think it's a good idea. An incentive program is wonderful, but some kids just don't daven loudly or shuckle a lot. That is not their fault. A grade for behavior during davening is okay, but a grade for davening is a poor idea.

Reward and Punishment — Incentives and Discipline

Bedtime by the Book

Q What is the proper time for my class of second-graders to go to sleep? In the nightly homework, should I have a box for the parents to check off if their son went to sleep by the recommended time? Or will that be a pressure for the parents to get the kid to sleep on time and will not be appreciated?

A 7:30/8:00 is a good time for second-graders to go to bed. While some parents will appreciate that being on the homework sheet to use as an incentive for their child to go to sleep on time, others might resent the pressure it puts on them. So it is up to you to decide whether to do it or not.

Discipline Without Pain

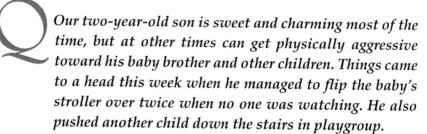 *Our two-year-old son is sweet and charming most of the time, but at other times can get physically aggressive toward his baby brother and other children. Things came to a head this week when he managed to flip the baby's stroller over twice when no one was watching. He also pushed another child down the stairs in playgroup.*

How do we get through to a child of this age that certain behaviors are not acceptable, from hurting his brother to "potching" his parents to purposely making messes, etc.? Are there times even nowadays when it is acceptable to give a potch to a young child? If not, what is an alternative that can be understood by a two-year-old, rambunctious boy?

Potching is certainly not the way to deal with this. You are attempting to teach a child that physical force is not okay by using physical force. That will teach him only that the physically stronger person wins. Instead, use the old-fashioned method of putting him in his room (or crib) until he comes out and apologizes, even if you have to do it ten times a day. Do not show *rachmanus* when it comes to hurting other people.

Bumps in the Road of Discipline

A while back, I spoke with Rabbi Bender about my child who was having a very hard time with discipline. At the time, you advised us to express disappointment without punishing. We tried that for some time and baruch Hashem, both he and we have come a long way.

Then, last night, we had to discipline him as he

ripped one of his brother's Circle cards on purpose. We told him he had to give his brother one of his, as that is only fair. Understandably, it was a very hard thing for him to do. He ultimately did give it to him, but in his anger, he took it out on me, attacking me both verbally and physically, hitting me many times. I told him I would give him a potch, and I did so in a very controlled manner, but that just escalated things. Finally, I raised my voice at him and he eventually calmed down. What should be the consequences of his actions? Did I handle it wrong? What can I do in the future?

A You have to look at your progress with your child as a graph. There will always be bumps in the road. But if in general you are seeing improvement and the graph is moving up, don't get stuck on a one-time event. If the *mehalech* you have been using has overall been working, continue doing what you have been doing and move on from this incident.

Avoiding the Trigger of the Word "No"

Q *Our six-year-old daughter responds drastically to the word "no." She is very aggressive and physical, bossy and manipulative. I know that all children have some difficult behaviors, but hers really get in the way of normal life. We were wondering if it was worth it for us to go to a parenting specialist for some tips on how to deal with her.*

A First try to leave out the word no. Instead, explain to her why something cannot be done at the moment, such as, "Oh my! That is not safe!" or "Please don't wake up the baby." Try to phrase everything without the word no. If that doesn't help, by all means, see a specialist.

Just Love Him

Q My teenaged son has been cutting school left and right. Today he slept through school, but he wants to go to his karate class. I want to say no! He says if he misses it, he may miss his chance to be promoted. I say life has consequences. What is your opinion?

A The short version: He is at risk. Smother him with love. Negatives will only push him away further. Especially at this age.

B. The long version: He is at risk. Smother him with love. Negatives will only push him away further. Especially at this age.

Counting on Good Behavior

Q I teach one subject to several classes. At the beginning of the year, I set up a contest with my classes where girls earn tickets for good behavior, and the class with the most tickets at the end of the term would get an ice cream party. At this point, it's pretty clear which classes deserve the ice cream party, but they don't necessarily have more tickets than the other classes, since different classes have different numbers of girls. I haven't counted the tickets, and that will be a very time-consuming and tedious job. Is it dishonest to just pick the classes with the best behavior without counting the tickets?

A Yes, I think that is dishonest. I don't think you have a choice. Give all the classes a party. You can tell them that there were too many tickets to count, but you cannot give them the impression that they were counted if they weren't.

Consequences of Nivul Peh and Bullying

Q *How would the Rosh Yeshivah deal with creating a policy for nivul peh (inappropriate speech)? What consequences should there be? What about bullying?*

Is it okay to impose a consequence for a student to have to go to a different class for a short while, or should there be a concern of embarrassing the child?

A It is very hard to make a policy on *nivul peh* or bullying. Every case must be decided separately. If, for example, a child comes from a home where there is *nivul peh,* you are not going to deal with him as harshly. If he comes from a very good home, you will be harsher.

The same is true for bullying. In our school, for both infractions, we have a minimum suspension of one day. That is, if a boy is fighting physically or using *nivul peh,* he is sent home. Then, depending on the situation and family, we add punishment if necessary.

It is not *l'chatchilah* to send a boy to another class, but if it must be done, send him to an older class, not a younger one, which is a punishment that hardens the criminal.

Is It a Punishment or an Option?

Q *My son has been coming home from camp with items that were not previously ours, telling interesting stories of how they came to be in his possession. After I verified that his stories were not true, he admitted he had stolen the items. I told him he had to return them to their owners and until he did, he could not return to camp and would have to spend the day sitting quietly in my office. He said okay, and we have so far spent one day together.*

I am afraid he will choose staying with me all day over returning the items. How should I proceed and how can I make sure it doesn't happen again?

A You may have made it sound like an actual choice, so he is choosing his preference. You must make it understood that returning the items is non-negotiable. After that, spend lots of one-on-one time with him. Take him out to eat, for walks, etc. During these warm get-togethers, bring up the topic of how people who steal young end up in jail when they are older. There are more dramatic steps you can take, but first try this. Let's daven and hope it will solve the problem.

Offering Incentives to Learn

Q *I am a tenth-grade rebbi in a mesivta. I maintain a very close relationship with my talmidim and their parents. The bachurim feel comfortable approaching me and discussing whatever is on their minds. However, this year, the dynamics of the class are such that ninety percent is academically compromised. Every day, it is a new struggle to engage them. For the most part, we are able to get them to "shtel tzu," but they would rather not be learning. We have discussed the fact that we need to shoulder responsibility even if we would rather be doing something else. We have spoken about the fact that even should one become a professional or businessman, he needs to have a solid foundation in Torah and yiras Shamayim. I try to create a fun and loving environment for my boys. Recently, they went out to eat on a Sunday night and they called me and asked me to join.*

Last month, the school brought in a V'haarev Na program for bekiyus. The boys sat with bottles of soda, nosh, and sushi and had a learn-a-thon for an hour and forty-five minutes. Upon completion, they were rewarded with a dinner of Chinese food. When I came to night seder that night, the boys said, "Rebbi! You try so hard to get us. Now you see what works!"

I am the only rebbi in my mossad who does not have programs or cut deals with my boys. I always feel the boys take advantage, and they learn not to put in effort if there is no carrot at the end of the stick. It has not affected my relationship with the boys. Many keep in touch with me for years, calling to shmooze in learning and general topics.

Can you please give me some sort of clarity to this age-old question? What is the definition of reward for learning? Regardless, should I apply the old adage, "If you can't beat 'em, join 'em"?

A The answer to this question is different depending on the *matzav* and situation. Rav Aharon Leib Shteinman says there is only one mitzvah that does not have a *mesorah*. *Chinuch*. Because the *derech* of *chinuch* changes depending on the situation and the generation. Go for it. Adapt to the *zman*. Times and methodologies change. If everyone around you is giving incentives, get on board!

Withholding the Laptop Can Backfire

Q *My son is fourteen years old and attends a chassidishe yeshivah. He's an average student. His father passed away when he was nine. He has seven married siblings and is the only child still living at home.*

He has a chavrusa with whom he connects and besides learning with him, he feels he can shmooze with him.

On a regular day, he goes to yeshivah before seven

and returns after eight. After night seder, he comes home and eats something, then he relaxes.

He has his own laptop, which does not have internet access. He likes playing with graphics software, for example, making photo montages of his family and watching Yiddish plays.

I have told him in the past that any non-Jewish videos or any video that has women in it is not allowed. Every few days, I go through his USBs (which the boys trade in yeshivah) to review and approve everything.

This past week, while he was out, I went through his USBs and found some unrated movies and TV shows. When he came home and asked for his laptop, I told him he could not have it because he broke the rules. I told him I need to think about what to do, but in the meantime, he cannot have the laptop back.

Since then, though he understands why I am withholding the computer, he is very angry. He cries and asks when he is getting the laptop back. Nothing else seems to calm him. I explained that I only want what's best for him, and how these things affect your neshamah. He is usually respectful of me, but now he says I am ruining his entire day because he knows when he comes home from a long day he cannot even relax with his laptop.

A The bottom line is, your son is correct, and you are wrong, in a way. Of course, really you are correct. But once your son has tasted *taam cheit*, it is very hard to stop him. Doctors say that computers and internet are as big an addiction as smoking and drugs.

Sure, he crossed you by lying to you. What else is new? He is a fourteen-year-old teenager growing up in the most difficult *dor* that I can recall. Forty years ago, when a boy wanted to see an inappropriate photo, he had to hang around the candy store and peek at the magazines. Today, all they have to do is push a button and, in the privacy of their own rooms, they can see the worst images. All the filters in the world cannot fully protect our children from this onslaught.

There are some programs that can help with this *yetzer hara*. They are worth looking into, but the boy has to want the help.

The bottom line is, you want to save your son. You cannot take away the laptop; he will get another one behind your back. Then you will have even less control. You must express your unstinting love for your son! *"Mein tiere kind*, you messed up. Okay. We will move on. I will let you have the laptop. But don't ever cross me again."

You are an *almanah*, but you are mature. He is a *yasom* and still immature. You must be the one to reach out. The goal is to save your son, not lose him.

Maintaining the Dress Code

Q We have upgraded our yeshivah's dress code to be more "yeshivish," but we are having difficulty with one boy who is finding it too difficult. Most significantly, he has been wearing very tight trousers, which Rabbi Bender advised us previously is something on which to draw the line as it is unsuitable.

At the moment, he has not returned to the zman as he was also not conforming to the seder hayom and fol-lowing the rules. We have told him he can return once he is ready to toe the line. We have, of course, been very accommodating in general, trying to help him, etc.

He wants to come back now and says he will try his best to follow the program. He has said that he will wear "a little looser" trousers, but won't budge any fur-ther than that. It is hard to know over the phone what he means by that. He wants to know if he can come back,

saying that if we are not happy, he will leave the yeshi-
vah. He cannot bring himself to budge any further, even
at the cost of his attendance here.

We feel a little blackmailed. Do we listen to him and
let him run the show? Or do we say he should only come
back when his mindset has changed? Otherwise, inevi-
tably, we are heading toward clashing with him, and it
will be uncomfortable if he returns and we need to send
him right back.

To summarize, there is a strong chance that when
he is asked to conform to looser-fitting pants, he will
say, "I prefer to leave the yeshivah." Do we allow him
to return?

No. You do not capitulate to him. He must conform completely; then he may come back. After all, you are not
asking for that much. A school has the right, and even
the obligation, to insist on children following the dictates of the
yeshivah. If he refuses, then you are not sending the child away;
rather, he is removing himself from your school. Schools must set
standards and enforce them.

Resist Peer Pressure
Regarding Tech Devices

Our son who is going into eighth grade is very easily
affected by those around him and always tries to fit in.
Baruch Hashem, he is doing very well in school and had
a wonderful rebbi last year.

Apparently, many boys in his grade have iPod
touches with texting/messaging and group chats. Our
son has been begging us to please get him an iPod touch
so he can join his friends. He feels very left out.

We do not want him to have an iPod touch, especially not with texting. Nowadays, one never knows what can happen. We are a pretty open-minded family in general. We travel with our kids, etc. But we do not think an iPod is necessary.

Should we give in to our son and let him get the iPod touch so he doesn't feel left out?

A Find another *eitzah* to get him something. You must give him something big, but not this! Tell him that is your decision and it is final. But find something else that he would enjoy and get him that.

Once More and He's Out

Q *A sixth-grader, with a history of lying and hanging out with the wrong crowd, approached a seventh-grader in the bathroom and showed him a smartwatch, saying, "Look at this video." The boy says it was clear from the thumbnail that it was adult content. The seventh-grader, a very good boy, told him to get lost. The sixth-grader tried again later and the seventh-grader refused again. The sixth-grader threatened that if he didn't watch it, he would teach his little brother a curse word. When the seventh-grader refused again, he carried through on his threat. Both kids came home shaken. What should be done with the sixth-grader?*

A The boy should be suspended immediately for a few weeks and warned that if anything remotely like this happens again, he must look for a new school. However, I'm not even sure you will be able to help him find a new school if he will hurt others like this. I am almost never a proponent of sending kids out of school. But where a child is ruining others, you must send him on his way and try to help him find a new school where he won't be hurting others. Teaching a younger brother a curse word is absolutely appalling! This is a case where the parents should be urged to consult a professional.

Accepted on a Strict Trial Basis

Q *There's a seventh-grade student in our school, a natural leader, who was using his leadership talents the wrong way and affecting other boys negatively, in the entire fourth through sixth grades. We have put him on probation, had meetings with his parents, etc. He's not a bad kid, but for our yeshivah and mission, due to his levels of outside exposure combined with his negative attitude about our school's mission and hashkafah, magnified by his natural leadership qualities, we felt that he was in the wrong environment. This past June, his parents enrolled his older brother in a Modern Orthodox high school that allows and even encourages student access to smartphones. To us, that confirmed that our school is not a fit for this family.*

At the end of the school year, I told the parents to enroll their son in a school more appropriate for his leanings. The parents did not apply to any school, hoping that I would change my mind. After this school year had already started, they applied to one school but were rejected. The boy is not in any school currently.

Obviously, this experience has been very difficult for the family and for the boy. The parents got very serious about improving his lifestyle, and they have assured me that things have changed dramatically. They tell me that they have cut off all access to technology and they no longer allow him to go to the park to play basketball with non-Jewish kids. They say they are committed to enrolling him in a yeshivah high school come next year. The parents do not have a good track record with honesty, so I can't confirm that all these claims are 100% accurate.

Members of our staff are concerned that, based on this boy's old behaviors, he will continue to have a negative influence on many of his classmates or on their choice of high school. The parents keep telling me that the boy has changed dramatically. He is not in school now and I am unsure what to do.

I am considering accepting him back under very strong conditions that are above and beyond our normal school rules: having absolutely no internet access, committing to enroll in a yeshivah high school, and signing a contract with detailed consequences that grow cumulatively with each offense.

A As I got to the middle of your email, I already wanted to write exactly what you propose. Give the boy a trial through June on probation with any conditions you want. You cannot risk the wellbeing of the entire student body, but at the same time, you cannot leave a child with no school to attend.

Revealing the Median Grade
Is a Positive Incentive

Q *I have been teaching tenth-graders for many years. A few years ago, I began a practice of telling my students the median grade of the class when returning a test. I felt this kind of feedback gave the students a type of "kinas sofrim" to achieve their best, and a way to gauge their performance in relation to the class. I also felt that this practice strengthened my position as a teacher. I was showing the students that this is a class where most students perform well and achieve. (The median was usually at about 85%.)*

This summer, I was speaking to a colleague who pointed out to me that, although this practice is advantageous to the upper 50% of performers, it may be discouraging or even cause feelings of shame for the lower performers.

I decided to ask my students. I handed out questionnaires to the current twelfth grade — my former students — asking them about this practice. The results were as follows: Of the fifty-four students in the grade, thirty-eight responded. Nineteen said they were above median and nineteen said they were at or below it. From those students who said they performed at or below the median, the response was overwhelmingly positive. There were, though, five negative responses. Two girls wrote that this made them "feel bad" because they knew that everyone was doing better than they were. The other three girls gave more neutral responses, saying that they were okay with it, but maybe other girls did mind it.

Considering the gain for the brighter girls and for most of the weaker girls, do I have to take into account the bad feeling this practice could generate in the one or two probably weakest — and therefore most vulnerable — girls in the class?

A You are doing the correct thing and it is wonderful. Even though I generally worry about the feelings of the weaker kids, I am also a very strong believer in positive reinforcement, which this really is. The weaker kids are not embarrassed; no one knows who they are. Why shouldn't they be pushed a bit? There are always a few kids who are very *shvach*, suffering all their lives, and we do care about these children, but this will not hurt them more.

The idea is wonderful. I will encourage all of our principals to do the same.

In the Classroom

Insisting on Clinical Evaluation

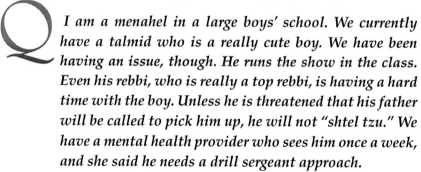

I am a menahel in a large boys' school. We currently have a talmid who is a really cute boy. We have been having an issue, though. He runs the show in the class. Even his rebbi, who is really a top rebbi, is having a hard time with the boy. Unless he is threatened that his father will be called to pick him up, he will not "shtel tzu." We have a mental health provider who sees him once a week, and she said he needs a drill sergeant approach.

Unfortunately, it is not working. He is sent out of class every day, and it has gotten to the point where the father himself is not holding up his end of the deal by picking him up and giving him what he needs. (The father himself is somewhat of a bully.) I don't want to send the boy to a place where he might get lost. If we ask the parents to evaluate him and give him what he needs, they will likely not follow through.

As a school, you have the right to demand that a child be tested or he cannot be allowed to return to school. I generally don't believe in throwing a child out, but if parents do not cooperate, the situation might need to be reevaluated.

Asking for a Different Morah

I am an almanah with one four-year-old son. This past year, he has been in nursery. Though his morah was kind and competent, I felt that she didn't really like him. My son is average to more leibedig. I believe he's on the brighter side and he has a lot of knowledge and loves to learn. I know he can sometimes cause trouble, but in general, he respects rules and thrives on consistency. The teacher said he can have a hard time sharing or waiting his turn, but that is to be expected as he is an only child and he gets all my attention and never has to share or take turns at home.

Apparently, toward the end of the year, my son had to be disciplined a lot. The teacher never reached out to me; I only know these things from reaching out to her. I spoke to the assistant who is a friend of mine, and she said she never saw this teacher show a negative opinion of my son.

Now this morah is moving up a grade, so my son will probably have her again if he goes into kindergarten. Should I request that he not have this morah?

Perhaps you are being oversensitive because of your own *matzav*, that of being a very young widow with one very young child. I would bet that the reason the morah didn't complain to you on her own about your child's behavior is that she didn't want to bother you. Your friend, the assistant morah, says all is fine. Leave things be just as they are and you will have a great year. He can certainly stay with his morah from last year. As you say, a lot of his behavioral issues likely have to do with the fact that he is the only child at home. I don't think you have anything to worry about.

Bikur Cholim During the Pandemic

Q My wife's brother is twenty-four years old. He has Down syndrome. He has been in the hospital on a ventilator for four weeks due to Covid-19. We are not confident about what the coming days will bring. My in-laws (who never ask for ANYTHING) very much want us to come for a Shabbos to visit him and to be with them.

Traveling out of state during the pandemic would mean that I would not be able to come back to my classroom for five days after my return. My menahel holds that it would be wrong for me to go. Considering the situation, I do not understand how I could just stay here. I want to just tell him that I am going and that's that. What should I do?

A This is not a *shailah* for me; this is a *shailah* for Rav Shmuel Kamenetsky. After conferring with him, he was quick and decisive. "You can't go. You can't go. You have a responsibility, and the *zechus* that you'll stay in your classroom will help him feel better more quickly." He said the same for your wife.

This question is not necessarily a Corona question. It comes up very often. As liberal and easy-going as I wish to be with the staff, I always felt that they must seriously consider when and if to take time off. As great as certain substitutes will be, we must realize that when a rebbi does take off, it means that there will be a very limited amount of Torah learned. And that should be the number-one question one should consider before he takes time off.

Matzah baking? *Brissim*? Child's event such as a *succah* fair? The list is endless. It needs major *machshavah*.

Drive-By Treats Help Maintain Morale

Q As mechanchos, we are trying to find our way in the present new normal. Our school is providing daily phone lessons and conference calls. We have arranged for school materials to be picked up once a month. For most of the students, this is satisfying and inspiring. We feel we are providing connection, stimulation, learning, and structure.

I wonder about the practice of schools distributing treats and gifts in drive-through settings. On the one hand, it maintains a nice connection, shows that the school cares, and brings good cheer to children and their parents. On the other hand, it seems to be driven somewhat by WhatsApp chats, with parents showing each other what their school did, what their niece's school in Monsey did, etc. It builds an expectation that their children should receive similar gifts.

Is it a valuable practice? Will we end up in a frenzy of trying to outdo other schools in proving to our parents that we also care?

A These are challenging times, and we must do whatever we can to keep an atmosphere of *simchah* in our yeshivos. In our yeshivah, we are hosting drive-bys where the *menahalim* and roshei yeshivah stand in the parking lot and wave to the kids in their cars. The first was on a Friday, and we distributed cholent and kugel to each family. On Lag BaOmer, we had singers and music blaring in the parking lot and distributed hot dogs and French fries to each *talmid*. I cannot begin to tell you how many letters of thanks we received. While the hand-outs are not absolutely necessary, though certainly very nice, the drive bys are a great idea. They keep the *simchah* and *ruach* alive during this difficult situation.

Modifying Schedule Due to Coronavirus

Q I am the menahel of a boys' mesivta and I am wondering about the start of the school year with Coronavirus. I am planning on starting with our regular schedule, including minyan (with social distancing) and breakfast. I am getting pushback from those who want to be very tight with all the bachurim and staff. They would rather have the boys daven before they come and just start from shiur. I am opposed to this idea. Firstly, many, many boys will not daven with a minyan, or even at all. Also, I am afraid that if we do not start the year with a regular schedule, it will be extremely difficult to switch from a modified schedule to a regular one. The boys get used to the modified schedule and there will always be a fear of the potential exposure to Coronavirus. Therefore, I think we should start with a regular schedule, and if chas veshalom we need to modify, we will. What are your thoughts?

A In our yeshivah, we are taking it easy the first week or two, breaking the boys in slowly. Our *minyanim* are super crowded so we are dividing sixth and seventh grades. But hopefully we will do this within ten days. Classes will start half an hour later because of distancing at breakfast. We have eleven hundred boys eating breakfast *bli ayin hara*, so we must modify somehow.

Must Zoom or Meet
With Social Distancing

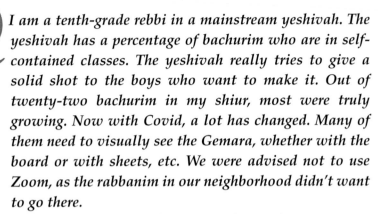

Q *I am a tenth-grade rebbi in a mainstream yeshivah. The yeshivah has a percentage of bachurim who are in self-contained classes. The yeshivah really tries to give a solid shot to the boys who want to make it. Out of twenty-two bachurim in my shiur, most were truly growing. Now with Covid, a lot has changed. Many of them need to visually see the Gemara, whether with the board or with sheets, etc. We were advised not to use Zoom, as the rabbanim in our neighborhood didn't want to go there.*

My question is what I can do at this point. Six bachurim are really shteiging; six don't even call in; the rest are doing the conference half-heartedly. I give two one-hour shiurim of which only half is Gemara. The stronger boys were getting upset that we weren't even doing Rashi, so I started to do that, but now I'm losing even the boys that got some outline of the Gemara, as it takes time for me to explain Rashi and for the boys to write down all the teitch.

In short, I am getting frustrated as to how little they're really learning. While I do know that the fact that most of them call in is itself amazing, I also feel bad for them and am fearful that there will be irreparable damage. We've done a huge incentive program that only resulted in rewards for the strongest boys.

A I understand that in your area, you are permitted to have ten people with social distancing. You should meet in person, half the kids, outdoors, ten in the morning, ten in the afternoon. They must see their rebbi. Nothing else will work with these kids. If this is not possible, use Zoom. It works magnificently. I do know of a few schools in your area using Zoom. With children such as you are describing, there is no *shailah*. But make sure to get the kZoom tablets that seem to be impenetrable; don't let them purchase their own.

Not Enough Teaching During Corona Pandemic

Q Some schools are doing a minimal amount of teaching over the course of each day. Should the parents pressure the schools to do more?

A An hour a day is not enough. That's where Zoom is useful, but I'm not pushing Zoom because it has its own problems. We use KZoom, which is restricted exclusively to school usage, so it can be used for longer periods of time. Speaking from a personal perspective, schools have been totally overwhelmed. It is always a major chore balancing the needs of twenty-five different children. What is good for one isn't necessarily what is good for the second child. In all my years in *chinuch*, this has been the most challenging time. Let's get through this just by trying our best and caring.

The question is if it is even possible for teachers to do more. The rebbeim and moros are working much harder teaching in a non-classroom setting, either via conference or Zoom. To push them harder is not going to work. One good thing that will come out of this *matzav* is that parents will see how hard rebbeim and teachers work. The amount of work that our rebbeim have done during Corona is absolutely incredible! Hats off to them!

Phone Conference Protocol

Q It can be challenging for kids to focus on the phone confer-
ences for class. Some kids are listening to them on roller-
blades. How rigid should parents be to get their children
to sit in one place with the phone as if they were in class?

A Let us first understand that the Zoom and conference
call issue is very much *b'dieved*. But my opinion is that
we should teach via conference/Zoom for twenty minutes at a time, during which time the students should be encouraged to take it seriously, and then give them a break and then
repeat the cycle. This pertains to younger children, and to *bachurim*
who struggle to learn in this manner. If they are learning at all, it's
an accomplishment. It falls to the mothers to monitor them and
they are very overburdened with household tasks simultaneously.
It is too much to ask that kids sit in front of a Zoom or telephone
as if they are in a classroom. So long as the kids are focusing, let
them be in whatever position they choose. Pick your battles.

Watching Zoom Classes

Q Our son is in kindergarten. Tomorrow he will start Zoom
classes. At home, our kids don't watch TV or movies of
any sort. We were a little hesitant to use Zoom, but were
advised that we should. How can I explain this to my
son? We never showed him any videos of any sort. Now
he will be using a tablet. How can we introduce the
device to him?

A I would tell him, "These are special times, and this is a
special rebbi video. Once you return to school, videos are
not for us." Seeing his rebbi live is not like watching any
other videos. Even at his age, he can understand the distinction.

Furthermore, the great danger we all face during these critical times is that our children shouldn't lose the *geshmak* of *Yiddishkeit.* Being away from the *ruach* that permeates the halls of a yeshivah can be devastating to many children. Some children simply don't have these "extras" available to them. We have no idea how long this pandemic will last. It is critically important that when yeshivos do re-open, our kids pick up right where they left off. The danger of being removed from Torah is far greater than the problems you worry about.

Let me just close by saying that you should feel very good that you have created a home that is clean of all outside influences.

Addressing Pandemic Discrepancies in Learning

Q When we open school, there will be a huge discrepancy in how well the children learned the material over the pandemic.

A Teachers must do a major *chazarah.* Some schools are considering letting the students begin the school year with the previous year's rebbi. Personally, I don't think that is a good idea. How will we handle the discrepancy of material covered between the classes? The rebbeim are fantastic and the children are resilient. It will be fine. Covering the material is not a problem.

The bigger challenge is to retrain them to be *talmidim* and observe proper classroom decorum. But as usual, everyone involved will come through in flying colors!

Who Has Priority?

Q When a menahel is speaking with a talmid and a rebbi wants to speak to him, should the menahel excuse himself and ask the talmid to wait, or should he finish with the talmid and then speak with the rebbi?

A There are two opinions on this. Personally, if my conversation with the boy will end quickly, I stop for a second and tell the rebbi I must finish with the *talmid*. It is critically important that once a *talmid* has my attention, I keep my focus on him. The only exception I make is for the Rosh Yeshivah. And even so, sometimes I tell him I will come to him soon. But if the conversation will be lengthy, I will tell the boy to wait a few minutes. Please remember that many boys have been waiting a long time to speak to their Rosh Yeshivah, *menahel*, or rebbi.

Challenges in the Classroom

Q I am the menahel of a boys' school and was hoping you could help me. We have a boy in third grade who is having emotional challenges with his rebbi. He gets triggered in a variety of ways. Things quickly escalate and he will literally have a tantrum — throwing things, mimicking his rebbi —and will not leave the classroom. At our insistence, the parents have an appointment to have him tested in a few weeks.

The tricky thing is that he performs well for his English teacher in the afternoon. She is very experienced, has very clear procedures, and the boy falls in line. The rebbi, on the other hand, is in his second year of teaching, is somewhat disorganized, and has less-than-perfect classroom management.

This week, the boy had a bad episode and had to go home. We decided he should stay out of school until his testing. The parents are asking if he could come for the afternoon, since he is doing well with his secular studies. I am reluctant to allow that because I am concerned about the impression it will make on the other boys. They have witnessed the boy acting disrespectfully to his rebbi. It's not a simple class to begin with, and I certainly don't want to complicate things for the rebbi.

A It is clear from your description that with an experienced rebbi, this boy would be okay. In our yeshivah, we hire a paraprofessional to sit with such a child during class. Find a way to keep him in school. Other kids are smart enough to understand that something is wrong and you are working on an *eitzah*. Children understand that exceptions are sometimes made.

Sometimes, when we have such a situation in our yeshivah, we will move kids around to a different class for the part of the day where things are not going well. If you have a few parallel classes, this can be done. The danger here, of course, is that the yeshivah becomes one big Grand Central Station with kids moving around. Also, parents may try to do this every year so they can have the perceived best rebbi and the perceived best teacher. That obviously will hurt the yeshivah. But occasionally, doing so can help you in a case like this. Not to be abused but can be helpful.

Disrespect to the Rebbi

Q *We had an incident today with an eighth-grade boy who has a track record of speaking disrespectfully to rebbeim and members of the hanhalah. Today, he was walking in the yard when he found a wad of chewed-up gum. He picked it up and aimed it at a rebbi, hitting his hat, where it stuck. When he saw he got a direct hit, he pumped his fist and shouted, "Yes!"*

I'm embarrassed such an incident ever took place at our yeshivah on my watch. We definitely put a strong focus on middos and derech eretz. But the boy comes from a challenging home environment, and his father had a heart attack a few months ago.

A I would probably suspend him for at least two weeks. Probably a month. And give him a final warning that one more infraction and he is out. You might now throw him out permanently, but children need to know that there are some boundaries one may never cross, and if one does cross them, there will be major consequences.

Chutzpah Is Unacceptable

Q *I have a seventh grade student who is very bright but who disregards the Limudei Kodesh teachers, getting Fs in all her classes. (In Limudei Chol she earns Bs and Cs, which are far beneath her ability.) She is unhappy, uninterested, defiant, and bringing others down. Her parents are divorced and life at home is unstable, but the mother has refused to get her therapy. We have tried anything and everything to allow her to shine, as she is extremely artistic and bright, but nothing has brought anything but the most superficial and short-term results.*

At this point, I question whether or not the student should remain in school. In all probability, if she leaves school, she will go to public school. But I am at a loss and the staff is very frustrated. The child is simply not interested in anything we have to offer.

A If the young lady is *chutzpadig*, and even with warnings continues to disturb the class by setting a bad tone, then you may not keep such a child in class if she refuses therapy. While the public school issue is unfortunate, your job is to protect your school. But try everything possible to save the girl before you send her away.

Punishing Questionable Chutzpah

Q *I am the principal of a Bais Yaakov junior high school, and I was wondering what I can do about the issue of chutzpah in my school. Sometimes I am not sure if what a girl said or did should be classified as chutzpah or not, and if it is, what is the proper way of dealing with it. The teacher affected by it wants the girl heavily punished. I do send girls home for very rude and blatant chutzpah, but there are times when there is a fine line.*

What if the teacher lost it and was acting kind of mean? How do I deal with teachers who get angry and cause a provocation?

A First of all, if you are not sure, then do not characterize something as chutzpah. Better to let chutzpah slide than to wrongly accuse an innocent child. There is certainly more chutzpah in today's age, but there was chutzpah years ago also.

Yes, it is different today. Years ago, when a child saw a morah or rebbi in the street, they ran the other way! Today, they run to say "Good Shabbos" and for the next few weeks will remind the teacher that they saw them outside yeshivah. So children treat their teachers much more casually today, and with that comes a familiarity that causes them to say things we wouldn't have dreamed of saying to a teacher years ago. The old style of *chinuch* does not work anymore. Yes, kids cross boundaries today. That does not mean we throw kids out of school or punish them heavily. What I am writing is not just my opinion; this was the opinion of Rav Shach and Rav Shteinman.

As to your second question, there is no place for meanness from a teacher. Such a person should not be teaching. Rav Moshe writes in *Parashas Emor* that if a rebbi cannot deal with issues, he should leave *chinuch*.

Bentching Without Bread

Q I work in an elementary school where the overwhelming majority of parents are baalei teshuvah. The children bring their lunches from home, and unfortunately, often do not bring bread. We have told them that anyone who didn't eat bread should bentch anyway and not say Hashem's Name, but we have noticed that they are saying Hashem's Name by mistake. If we don't practice bentching in school, these kids will likely never learn it and will struggle with it later. What should we do? We cannot force the children to eat bread. Is it a problem if they are saying Hashem's Name by accident if it is for chinuch purposes?

A It would be a nice idea to have bread available in the classroom for the children. Yes, if they don't want bread, they should *bentch* anyway. They must learn how to *bentch*.

Encouraging Bircas HaMazon

Q I have observed that when lunchtime comes, almost no one in my class washes, and therefore, almost no one bentches. I am afraid that on Shabbos, these boys will *not know how to bentch because they rarely do it during the week. Is this an area where I should step in, perhaps creating a program for netilas yadayim and Bircas HaMazon while they're still young, or is this a place in which I should leave well enough alone?*

One cannot fight the world. The fact of the matter is, kids today are no longer interested in washing. The children who get hot lunch look at the main dish, but are not interested in the bread. This is also true in camps. When I was young, we *bentched* three times a day in camp. It was *leibedig* and *freilech* in the dining room. The *niggun* used for *bentching* still reverberates in my head. Kids had no problem *bentching* after all three meals.

Were you to visit camps today, you would find that at nearly all meals, the head counselor or dining room counselors will sing or say *Al HaMichyah* with the children if they ate *mezonos*. Unless rolls were served during breakfast or hot dog buns at supper, they rarely *bentch* together.

Is this good? Of course not. Kids should learn how to *bentch*. But we cannot fight reality.

As long as you are able to get them to *bentch* together, that's great. But when it does not go well, throw in the towel. *Iy"H*, one day, they will learn how to *bentch*.

By the way, I know some wonderful *mishpachos* who sing the Shabbos and Yom Tov *bentching* together. Encourage your parent body to do so. That will take care of the issue.

Thank you for being such a wonderful and dedicated rebbi.

Davening With the Class

I am the dean of a yeshivah and I have a question for Rabbi Bender. There is a boy in our eighth grade who is very shtark in his Yiddishkeit and committed to extra learning and avodas Hashem. I am doing my best to be *mechanech him in a healthy and balanced way, as he has a tendency to take things over the top. Early this year, he asked me about "sneaking" in some Torah learning during general studies classes. I had him discuss it with his family and Rav, and it was decided that it was not something he should do.*

Recently, he asked me if he could daven at an earlier minyan than we have in yeshivah. He reasoned that if he davened at a 7:15 minyan, he could learn from 8:00-9:15 when classes start here. Beyond the ramifications for this boy, we do not have such a large eighth-grade class, and having him at minyan is good for the school. At the same time, I understand that he wants to learn extra, certainly a good thing.

A You are correct that it is best to be healthy and normal. He should daven in school. Explain to him that it is counterproductive to be different. In a large school or with special circumstances, there might be room to make an exception. This is not a special circumstance.

This age can be somewhat risky and one doesn't want too much pressure put on a child. On the other hand, this is self-induced pressure. So, you are working with a double-edged sword. Use good judgment while weighing all the circumstances.

Nipping Stealing in the Bud

Q *We had a situation recently where a five-year-old stole money from his teacher's pocketbook. (We saw this on the cameras so we know for a fact that it happened.) What would be a teachable consequence to help him with such a mistake and ensure that it does not happen again?*

A Five years old is very young. You must have a conversation with him one on one about what it means to hurt others. I would tell him a story. Something like: "Maybe morah has little kids at home and she had money in her pocketbook to buy them bread and milk. Because you took the money, the kids went to sleep without supper."

Generally speaking, when children steal, they do not think about the damage they cause. In general, children are kind. When you teach them how they are hurting others, it goes a long way, especially at this age.

Skipping One Grade, Not Two

Q We have a first-grade girl in our school who is very advanced, both academically and socially-emotionally. She happens to be taller than her peers as well. Her parents have been discussing the possibility of having her skip a grade and enter the third grade this coming year instead of the second. The grade above her current grade has a different dynamic that we don't feel would be beneficial to the girl. Therefore, we are considering possibly moving her up two grades into the fourth. I do feel that, even after moving up two grades, she will be successful socially, emotionally, and academically. However, I'm concerned about the long-term ramifications down the line once her classmates reach adolescence.

I have never skipped a child two grades before; however, she is not accomplishing much in school right now. Her parents are concerned that if she stays put, she will get accustomed to feeling as if she is wasting her time and talents and lose motivation.

A I would not skip a child two grades. As you said, when her classmates reach adolescence, she will be a baby. Girls of that age can be very catty and will make fun of her. Skipping a grade is not a simple matter. If you must skip her at all, do one grade only.

Punished for ADHD

Q *My son has a tremendous amount of koach and a tremendous amount of chein. He is incredibly smart but has always been impulsive, with lots of energy, etc.*

Despite his intelligence, he has struggled through school. He has a hard time focusing, sitting still, and paying attention, and he gets into fights at recess. He would always come home with a sob story of what happened that day, but his rebbeim often have a different story to tell.

Over the years, I have discussed the possibility of his having ADHD with his pediatrician, who advised us to leave it alone. Last year, though, things came to a head when my son started doing things that were clearly dangerous to himself and others. The doctor finally agreed to put him on medication. Suffice it to say that it has been a very long haul trying to find the right medications and doses.

We finally got him onto a medication that seems to be working and have been slowly adjusting the dosage. Baruch Hashem, this past month has been like techiyas hameisim for him in terms of how he feels about school and how he is performing.

Until yesterday.

Yesterday he woke up late and in the rush to make the bus, forgot his medication.

From the start of the day, he was antsy, fidgety, etc. The rebbi kept trying to refocus him but nothing worked. He ended up losing his recess and getting an assignment. He was very upset and when the rebbi's back was turned, he made a rude gesture. Some of the boys laughed and when questioned they told the rebbi what my son had done. The rebbi asked my son if he had taken his medication. When my son said no, he sent him out for a few minutes and then brought him back in with nothing else said.

However, the menahel called me last night incredibly upset. He said my son would have to stay home for a bit. He did not say for how long.

When we told our son last night, he was crying and then incredibly angry. He blamed the school, the rebbi, etc. We explained that we love him, but that he cannot be chutzpadig, to the rebbi. This morning, he was much more subdued and sad. I feel like we had come so far and this is such a setback.

My husband and I are unclear if this was right or wrong on the part of the rebbi and the yeshivah. I feel like, you know the child has ADHD and he has been perfect for the last month. Why didn't you call me? Ask if he took his medication? Why wait until it gets out of hand? It's only normal for a child to forget his medication once in a while. Then again, I understand their point of view. He did act out, and worse, made his friends laugh at the rebbi.

I'm worried about my son's self-esteem and the trust that has been broken between him and his rebbi. How can it be repaired?

We are very torn here between just hugging my son and validating him, or standing firm and telling him what he did is not okay. Ultimately, I know he has to take responsibility for his actions, but I feel like right now, so much is not in his control.

A There are many different points in this letter. First, you are to be commended for trying to get the child onto medication. Mostly the opposite is true. Parents sometimes fight meds, which often hurts their child. I don't believe that the answer to all issues is meds. Absolutely not! But there is a time for everything. The fact that you are not running away and, in fact, are being very supportive is wonderful.

The second point is how the school should handle issues. Based on what you described, the rebbi was wonderful. He understands *chinuch*. He understands that certain circumstances can cause a child to act out in a disrespectful way. This is not an uncommon occurrence with kids who are on medication. The rebbi handled it perfectly, but I don't understand the *menahel's* actions. If things were under control, why create a new *tzimmes*? I would understand the *menahel* reacting badly if the story happened when he was there and he didn't know the extenuating circumstances. But after the fact? As for you, you must give your son *mussar* with one hand, and be *mekarev* him with the other. He must know he made a major mistake, but life goes on. He should return to yeshivah as soon as he is able. This is an everyday story. Do not worry. *B'ezras Hashem*, he will come around.

Parents' Divorce Affecting Son's Learning

Q I am hoping you can help me with one of my students. He is extremely bright and has been in an accelerated Gemara shiur for some time. He used to love learning and loved this rebbi's shiur, which is very engaging.

Now his parents are in the midst of a very contentious divorce and he is pulling away and shutting down. He performed very poorly on his last two exams. I don't see how I can keep him in the accelerated shiur at this rate.

A This is always a very difficult question. Kids from divorced homes suffer more than any other.

There are two things I would do. First, I would try to arrange for him to have a mentor/big brother/*chavrusa* to learn with him, take him out to eat, and be his best friend and someone he can talk to. Second, I would find the boy a job within the yeshivah. Kids from divorced homes suffer from a terrible loss of self-esteem. They are embarrassed by the fights of their parents. When you give him a job in yeshivah, going around to classes taking attendance or the like, he will feel better and be better able to learn.

Dangers of Social Media

Q *I am the principal of a yeshivah with a parent body that spans a wide spectrum of frumkeit. They are mostly baalei teshuvah and are holding at different points in their journeys. We are currently having an issue with smart devices. Many of our parents use them, but only a small percentage have filters. Moreover, many of them have begun buying devices for their children as young as sixth grade. Some of these children are already on social media. How do we nip this in the bud?*

A There are many public schools today that do not allow phones in school. There is literature on the dangers of smartphones in general and social media in particular — especially for the young mind — that you can distribute to your parent body. You do not have to make this a religious issue. You can set a school policy based on educational research.

Child Suffering
Due to Parent's Incarceration

Q *The father of one of my talmidim was convicted of a white-collar crime, and he's beginning a two-year prison sentence tomorrow. The boy started off the year well, but since his father's sentencing, he's understandably been spiraling downward in both his academics and his behavior. Apparently, most of his classmates know; it is not a secret in his community. There have been a number of instances when other boys made very insensitive comments, which I dealt with as quickly and firmly as I could. My question is, how should I proceed with him moving forward while keeping the equilibrium in the classroom? I want to give him some leeway, but I can't let it get to the point where he's the obvious nebach who gets away with things. On the other hand, I feel like I can't be tough, either.*

A This is not easy. I have always felt that children, even from the ages of seven, eight, and on, are very sensitive to other children's personal issues. It is absolutely terrible that the community at large knows about the incarceration. But the one advantage you have is that since the kids know that all is not well in that household, you can give this *talmid* a lot more attention. The children will understand, like they understand a child who is a *yasom* or even from a single-parent home. Let's give this kid the benefit of the doubt at all times, even if we don't do that with his classmates.

HaRachaman … B'Gan Eden

Q *One of my third-grade students is a yasom, and I was wondering what to do during bentching when we reach the phrase, "HaRachaman Hu yevareich es avi mori"? Do we say it and risk hurting this boy? Or do we all just say, "kol hamesubin kan" and skip the part about parents?*

A The Munkatcher siddur says that one can continue to say this *HaRachaman* even after his parents are no longer alive. Some say that it is appropriate to add *"b'Gan Eden"* at the end. This world is just a stopover. Our parents continue to live on. You may explain this privately to your student. Then you can say the *HaRachaman* with your class.

I am a Munkatcher chassid for this one mitzvah. I have always said *HaRachaman Hu yevareich es avi mori v'es imi morasi b'Gan Eden*. I now also add *HaRachaman hu yevorech es avi chumi v'es imi chamosi b'Gan Eden*. What is wrong with that? It makes me feel better and it will make your *talmid* feel better.

Even a Yasom Must Behave in School

Q *I have a yasom in my sixth-grade class who lost his father just over a year ago. At the beginning of the year he was very quiet and did not participate. I was very nice to him and tried to speak to him outside of class about topics that interest him.*

However, lately he has begun misbehaving in class. I do not know what to do. I do not want to cause any more pain to this boy, but misbehaving is not acceptable. What should I do?

A This is a tricky question, and I shared it with the distinguished *menahel ruchani* of Yeshivah Tiferes Zvi in Chicago, Rabbi Nosson Muller. In general, you must use as much *ahavah* as possible. *Chitzoniyus meorer es hapnimiyus* (our external actions influence our internal emotions) is not only in dress. It is in relationships as well. Overload the boy with love outside the classroom. Give him time, treats, invite him for Shabbos meals, etc. But in the classroom, there need to be boundaries. You cannot allow him to abuse his *yasmus*. There is nothing wrong with discipline as long as he is not embarrassed in public. Let's hope that eventually, the *chitzoniyus* out of the classroom will affect his behavior in the classroom.

Treating Yesomim Differently

Q *I'm a leibedig kind of guy in class, and my rebbi is very tolerant of me. One time, when I wasn't present and boys asked my rebbi why they get punished when I don't, he told them that it's because I'm a yasom. This really annoyed me. He should treat me like anyone else! I haven't spoken to him since.*

A I think that you are wrong on this. There is nothing wrong with other boys knowing that you are a *yasom*. They don't know what it means to live through being a *yasom*, what it means not having a father at the Shabbos table, not having someone you can rely on to help with homework. They don't know. There's nothing wrong with the rebbi telling the class. Not because you are a neb. You are not. But because they should know what you are going through. And yes, you deserve to be treated differently because of it.

The Torah tells us that *Hakadosh Baruch Hu* is the *Avi Yesomim*. I was a *yasom* just like you and I didn't like being treated differently, but the Torah tells us that we have to treat *yesomim* differently. My father, *zt"l*, in his *shmuess* as *menahel* at Torah Vodaas, used to describe what it is like to be a *yasom* by explaining that it is the difference between getting a smack on a healthy hand versus getting a smack on a hand with an open wound. That's what it is like to be a *yasom*. Things hurt that much more.

You want to be regular. That is fine. And it is fine if you don't want to make a tumult about your status. But when you are not around, it is fine for your rebbi to do so, because that is the fact. There is nothing wrong with what the rebbi did.

When a visiting Rav comes to Yeshiva Darchei Torah, I always introduce the *yesomim* personally. I treat them better, and I want them to get a special *berachah* when a big *tzaddik* comes. Look at this boy who lost a parent and is still a *ben Torah*!

Referring to Loss in the Classroom

Q I have a boy in my class who lost his mother two years ago and is still suffering. Do I have to be careful not to ever mention references to shivah homes or any similar topic?

A You should always remain cognizant that he is in your classroom, but it is impossible to completely skirt the issue. You and your classmates should make every effort to be as careful as possible. But don't feel guilty if you mess up a bit.

Keep the Talmid in Yeshivah

Q There is a young man in our yeshivah who has been causing all kinds of grief. It has become impossible for the rebbi to teach when he is in the room. He is bringing the other boys down with his behavior and I would like to expel him, unless you have advice to the contrary.

A I know the boy in question and he is a yasom. If you expel him, he will be labeled for life. Please allow him to complete the school year and then find him another yeshivah. Even if he makes the worst tzaros, I don't think you can send away a yasom. None of this is chas veshalom mussar. You must be putting up with a lot if you are even considering sending him away.

We have our share of such situations in our yeshivah, but based on a psak from Rav Aharon Leib Shteinman many years ago, we never send any child away from yeshivah unless and until we find him another place to attend. The Brisker Rav never turned down a yasom who applied to his yeshivah. He was afraid of the *din v'cheshbon* in the *pesukim* in *Parashas Mishpatim*. I will work with you by speaking with the boy constantly to check in and be *mechazek* him. Please find it in your heart to allow him to finish the year.

Inappropriate Activities Can Lead to Expulsion

Q *I am the menahel of an elementary-school yeshivah. There is a boy in fourth grade who is apparently being exposed to some highly inappropriate things. I am not fully clear on the situation. However, what is clear is that both parents are working, and the child is in his grandmother's house with a cousin who is definitely exposed to television and the internet.*

A I would call in the parents immediately for a meeting. Tell them what you know. If the boy continues to be exposed, he may not stay in yeshivah. If they don't want to have a son who is crippled for the rest of his life, they must act quickly. Be as sweet as you can, but don't budge.

Rebbi Is Out of Line

Q *I live in an out-of-town community and my son's rebbi from last year is a real hands-on learning type, keeping the boys engaged and interested.*

However, he is also a "shtick macher," and defies school rules openly. For example, when the menahel asked them not to leave the sefarim on the tables where they were learning, the rebbi moved each sefer to a different table (instead of putting them away, which was clearly the menahel's intent). Not a great way to teach the boys derech eretz. Things like this happened throughout the year.

I'm concerned because my next son will have this rebbi this year. Should we speak with the rebbi openly and tell him we don't agree with his lack of derech eretz and not following rules? We don't want to put a rebbi down. Should we discuss it with the hanhalah? It's a small community. If he loses his job, everyone will hear about it and he may not get another. Should we tell our son that we don't agree with what the teacher does?

A rebbi should not lose his job over this, but he certainly must be spoken to. However, you are correct that it should not come from parents. The *hanhalah* must speak to him. On the other hand, do NOT discuss this with your son. If an issue develops during the year, worry about it then.

The Right Way to Discuss Technology

One of the rebbis in our school wanted to eradicate smartphones from his class. He offered to buy their phones from them, and then they had a phone-smashing "party." He gave a shmooze about phones this week, speaking of their evils. I feel in a school where most of the parents have such devices, it is incorrect to use such harsh language and methods.

You are correct. This is absolutely not our *derech*. What a rebbi should say is that in the wrong hands, a smartphone can be a very big problem. In today's time, many people need an iPhone for business or the like. But for a *bachur* who has a *yetzer hara*, this device can be poison.

He Belongs in His Father's Class

Q My son is finishing seventh grade in the school where I am one of the eighth-grade rebbeim. In our yeshivah, the boys are split into three streams according to their academic ability. My son is currently in the higher class, as he is baruch Hashem bright and enjoys the challenge.

I teach the higher class in the eighth grade. What is better for my son? Should he be in my class where he will be with his friends and in a class that meets his academic needs, or should I put him in the middle class where he won't have his father as a rebbi but will have to make new friends?

A Unless your son is super-sensitive and will get upset if someone says something not nice about the rebbi, he belongs in your class with his friends. But make sure not to be tough on your son just to show that you don't play favorites. That wouldn't be fair to your son.

Adding Additional Night Seder
to the Schedule

Q We have started a new yeshivah, now in its second year. We have a ninth and tenth grade. Our school day starts at 7:45 a.m., with Shacharis, and General Studies ends at 7:00 p.m. It's a long day, and for that reason, last year we had night seder only once a week. The boys would stay after school and have supper from 7:00–7:30 and then have seder until 8:15.

I am wondering what to do this year, now that we have a tenth-grade class. Seeing as the day is so long, should we do the same for them like last year? Or is it necessary to add something for the tenth-grade boys?

A It would be nice to do night *seder* two nights a week if your *bachurim* are ready for it. In our yeshivah, we had two nights and then moved to three nights weekly, with many boys staying 4-5 nights a week. This is now becoming more and more the accepted standard in our yeshivah world. If you choose not to go along, you may be deterring certain children whom you want to apply to your yeshivah.

Out of the Classroom

Derech Eretz Out the Window

Q Our eighth-grade boys went on a graduation trip. On the bus ride back, several boys threw things out the window, making a real chillul Hashem. Some boys also had a water fight at the back of the bus, completely ignoring the rebbi who told them to stop. What disciplinary action should be taken, and which avlah should be stressed?

A This has always been a difficult problem. On the one hand, they deserve to be smacked (so to speak, not to be taken literally). On the other hand, you don't want eighth-graders to leave with a sour taste. You want them to stay close to you and close to yeshivah. This is an issue in all yeshivos. Trips are at the end of the year when kids are already restless.

I would give them a very strong *shmuess* on *chillul Hashem*, and tell them if they were not graduating, you would come down much harder on them.

Using Funds Raised for Cancelled Trip

Q The students in my class raised money during the year by building succos, raking leaves, running a raffle, selling snacks, etc. to fund an end-of-year trip with their rebbi. Unfortunately, with Covid, the trip does not seem likely to happen. The question now is, what should be done with the money that was raised? We could try to find ways to spend some of it on a catered dinner of some sort, but what about the rest? Should the students receive some of it as compensation for missing their trip? Or is that not appropriate since they were paid this money by people thinking it was funding a trip for the boys to enjoy and grow from?

A A catered dinner with their rebbi sounds like an excellent idea. If there is money left over, perhaps a gift can be bought for each boy. Donors will be understanding of the situation. Or maybe things will open up later in June. But giving the boys the money is in poor taste.

Electronic Games Don't Belong in School

Q What is the Rosh Yeshivah's opinion on children bringing electronic games (Nintendo and the like) to school to play with during breaks or recess? (Obviously, so long as the games are "kosher.")

A This is a terrible thing. It is a bad lesson for the kids. There are other games to play. Children should be interacting with each other and getting fresh air, playing sports or board games, even tic-tac-toe! There should be no electronic games in school.

Racism Is Unacceptable in Any Form

Q My seventh-grade son was unfortunately suspended from his bus for joining his friends in singing a song laced with racial slurs to the bus driver. What should be our reaction? How can we drive home a sense of kavod habriyos and derech eretz?

A You must sit him down and give him a *shmuess*. And take something away from him. Don't be too harsh, but he must understand the severity of his actions. They must know the consequences of *chillul Hashem*. Their actions can affect the bus driver's attitude to *Yiddishe kinderlach* forever!

Additionally, they must understand that according to most of Chazal, everyone, yes, everyone has a *tzelem Elokim*. Making fun of a person born with a different color is the same as making fun of a handicapped individual. When we mock anyone, we are hurting our *neshamos*. All people are created by *Hakadosh Baruch Hu*, and by poking fun at different types of people we are mocking Hashem's creations.

Can we imagine Rav Moshe Feinstein acting racist? Or the Chazon Ish? Or Rav Shach? Never! The boys should write an apology to the bus driver and hand it to him. A representative of the school should speak to the driver as well.

All Tied Up

Q I am a rebbi in an out-of-town yeshivah. There has been discussion among my peers as to whether we should be wearing a tie at all times; i.e., even when not in yeshivah. The accepted practice has been not to wear ties after yeshivah hours, but there are those who feel that since we are a small community and are never truly "off the *clock," we should wear a tie consistently throughout the school year. Is this the proper thing to do?*

You have a problem in your neighborhood. When heads of schools don't wear ties, others will not. My feelings are that *l'chatchilah* you should wear a tie, but *nisht gefer-lech* if you don't. There are some rebbeim who do not wear ties after school. Some people do not respect them as much. I don't think respect should be contingent on a tie, but these are the facts.

Dealing With a Talmid's Illness

I am the rebbi of a boy who has recently been diagnosed with cancer. I do not know how to react. Beyond calling, should I visit him? What do I say to a talmid who is staring death in the face? Or to his devastated parents?

You can tell your *talmid*, "Hashem gave you a *nisayon*. It is a difficult one. You are not well, but this world is full of nonstop *nisyonos* that can be very difficult. But the people who make it in this world are the ones who overcome *nisyonos*. Call on me to help you if you are afraid. I will try to ease your pain in the best way I can. Don't feel sorry for yourself, it is not a healthy outlook." It would be good to seek guidance from Chai Lifeline. They are experts.

There is also nothing wrong with a rebbi telling his *talmid*, "I have also gone through pain, and looking back, I grew dramatically from my experiences."

WhatsApp Chat With the Entire Class

Q *Can a rebbi have a WhatsApp group with his talmidim to be used to give them chizuk if it is all done outside of school?*

A If every single student has WhatsApp, then it may be fine. I cannot say for sure, but maybe it is always wrong for a rebbi to WhatsApp with his *talmidim*. There are some who believe they should never, ever text! However, many good rebbeim text with children today.

However, if any student in the class does not have WhatsApp, it should not be done. It is not fair to leave a child out for doing what is considered the preferable thing.

Night Seder America Is Beneficial

Q *My son had a great year last year in seventh grade. He started learning Gemara with geshmak and that continued until Covid-19 hit. Since then, he is out of routine and has not been able to keep up with learning on the phone. I just discovered Night Seder America, which is on Zoom, and he liked it. Would it be okay to get him a tablet just for Zoom to use for Night Seder America and other such things? It would, of course, be filtered and only under my supervision.*

A It is perfectly fine to allow your son to use such a device under supervision. Night Seder America is a terrific program. It is very special and very positive for your son to join.

*I*n a
Social Forum

A Nachas Note

My wife and I asked you years ago if we should encourage our sensitive and sweet six-year-old son to befriend the quieter, unpopular boy in his class, or to seek out friends more his type; i.e., the athletic, fun, popular boys. You advised us at the time that telling our son to do a chesed will never be the wrong thing.

I wanted to let you know that my wife recently met a mother of a boy in our son's class, a quiet, reserved boy, and the mother told my wife that her son does not really have a lot of friends but he told her that he wants to give mishloach manos to our son, not because they're such good friends, but because our son is a nice boy!

So thank you for your advice all those years ago.

Thank you so much for sharing this story with me. It's a source of *chizuk*. Continue being wonderful parents!

It's Time to Step Up and Reach Out

Q Let me first remind Rabbi Bender of our situation. We live in a development with several frum families. There is a neighbor who was exposing our girls to dangerous and inappropriate concepts. In her home, there are movies all the time, not only non-Jewish, but not kosher as well. The girl is also somewhat of a bully, insisting on playing in her house because "it's the best," shaming others, etc. Most of the other parents have forbidden their daughters from playing with this girl, but I feel bad for her as she will be left with no friends in the development. Rabbi Bender was so kind as to meet with the parents of the girl, and they sent a text to all the neighbors assuring us that they will mend their ways.

But a text is not enough. I am leaning toward separating my daughter from this girl as well. I am torn between concern for this young girl and her family, and on the flipside, protecting and sheltering my daughter.

A Separating your daughter at this juncture would be very unfair, halachically wrong, and extremely *unmentchlach*. You came to me with a problem. I traveled far from home to meet with the couple. I spoke with them until late at night. They were *mekabel* to correct their ways. Of course, they were defensive, but they realized they must do something. They sent a text to this effect to their neighbors.

The rest of you should be reaching out to them now. Do the right thing! Good thing you don't run a yeshivah; you would throw out all the kids! Forgive me for being so *sharf*, but I feel for this family. In addition, you should know that you cannot run away from these issues in this day and age. It could happen to you again, in school or in your new neighborhood with someone else.

You did the right thing by telling me. We are dealing with it. Give the kid a chance now. If you do, *Hakadosh Baruch Hu* will help you be *matzliach* with your children.

Do Not Disturb!

Q *I live in an upstairs apartment and have several young children. My three-year-old son and five-year-old daughter tend to wake up very early, and the elderly neighbors downstairs have complained about the noise they make. We have tried various things to keep them quiet in the mornings, including letting them watch kosher videos, but I am not happy with the amount of screen time they are getting. How can I make sure they don't yell and make a ruckus in the morning?*

A I really feel for you. I understand your neighbors, but you cannot keep such young children quiet. Many have tried and failed. It is okay to let them watch kosher videos to keep them quiet, but that can only be used for a short period of time. You should definitely try other things to keep them occupied. Get them stickers, coloring books, etc. Perhaps that will buy you some time in the mornings. You should also train them not to play over the neighbors' bedroom during sleep time, and not over the dining room during mealtime.

Petitioning for Change

Q *The shul where I learn and daven has been part of the community since the dawn of time. It was started by the current Rav's grandfather. Before the kollel came to the shul four years ago, it almost closed due to lack of attendance. Now that the kollel has come, and many other young people have bought houses in the neighborhood, there is a window of opportunity to change many facets of the shul to cater to the younger, more yeshivish crowd.*

The problem is, many people are still reluctant to daven there for several reasons. They say the Rav's derashah is too long, his Shemoneh Esrei is too long, he likes to do everything himself and doesn't delegate, he is too old school, and other such complaints. It has come to a point where more and more young people are choosing to daven elsewhere, and we are left with only the kollel members who are required by contract to daven in the shul.

To his credit, the Rav has made several changes and wants to cater to more people. He has expressed his confusion as to why more people still do not daven there. I and a few others have spoken with the Rav about the issues and nothing has changed.

I was considering getting fifteen people to sign a petition concerning the issues in the hopes that the Rav would see that they are serious issues and not just complaints of a small few.

A You have a problem and you need to find ways to make the shul and the Rav more relevant. Changing a person is very difficult. Your issue is a real issue today in most communities. It is for that reason that when a new shul opens up with, say, thirty-year-olds, by the time fifteen years go by, the new thirty-year-olds make their own shul. They feel that they are not welcome to the club or that the Rav is not understanding of the young ones. The answer to this issue is for the entire shul to work together to ameliorate the situation, but if the Rav doesn't go along, forget it.

But never, ever write a petition against the Rav. It is appalling for members of a shul to give *mussar* to the Rav. How dare a forty-year-old, possibly an *am haaretz* who at best learns a quick *daf yomi*, give *mussar* to a *talmid chacham*?! You are not happy. Try quietly to bring change, or go elsewhere!

Never do something *chutzpadig* to a Rav.

"Please Dress Appropriately"

Q I have a good friend who is becoming progressively less *frum*. Her husband and my husband are also good friends (but he is in a better place hashkafically). We live on the same block and our kids play in each other's houses. The problem is, she no longer dresses in a tzniusdig fashion, and we are wondering if this is a problem regarding our children's chinuch. Our eldest daughter is almost five. My husband is also uncomfortable when my friend comes to our home dressed in a way that is not tzanua.

A There is nothing wrong with telling her that she should please dress in a *tzniusdig* manner when coming to your apartment, or even when your kids are at hers. She is clearly not a person who simply doesn't know better. Your husband is correct. Sometimes we need to do the uncomfortable thing and speak to people about certain *inyanim* that make us uncomfortable. Obviously, this must be done in a very *eidele* way. We mustn't forget that *"Deracheha darchei noam* — Its ways are ways of pleasantness."

Stirring Up Trouble With the Neighbors

Q I live on a dead-end block, and the children often play outside unattended. Lately, I have been told by a neighbor that my two daughters (six and seven) and a friend have been excluding her daughter (I'll call her Sarah) from their games. This was going on for a while, but things seem to be getting worse. Sarah's mother told me *that my daughters spilled soda into her pool. None of the other mothers saw it happen and none of the suspects owned up to it, but I cannot dismiss it out of hand.*

The next morning, Sarah's mother was very friendly, chatting about her niece's upcoming wedding and sheva berachos she was making, etc. Later though, Sarah and her siblings told me that "a robber" threw garbage into their yard and it broke something. They didn't know who did it because no one was home at the time. I asked my kids if anyone had been near Sarah's house. One older daughter told me she saw my six- and seven-year-olds in the backyard and she heard one of them say, "Okay, you can go to Sarah's house now."

I do not want to accept such rumors/third-hand lashon hara, but since my girls seem to be suspects and I know they are not always innocent, I feel that I need to do something.

What complicates matters is that Sarah's family, while nice, frum neighbors, sometimes seem to be asking for a fight. They may tag along or bother other kids. Sarah's mother may insist that her children be included, even if it is her five-year-old boy with all the seven-year-old girls. How can we restore and keep shalom with Sarah's family?

A You must tell the children that if they cannot play nicely outside, they will have to remain inside the house all the time. It is that simple. There must be real consequences if you want this to stop. It will not go away by itself. Because you are living in such close proximity, this is a long-term situation and you must nip it in the bud. You should also discuss this openly with your neighbor. Together, you should come up with guidelines of what it is reasonable to expect from the girls. (To include Sarah, who is also seven, in their play is reasonable. Not wanting a five-year-old boy to tag along is also reasonable.)

Switch Back

Q I run a large day camp in the Tristate area. A parent called me and asked that Chaim not be in her son Yossi's bunk because he has bullied him in the past. I did a quick switch and put Chaim in a different bunk. I didn't realize the counselor had already made his introductory call. Chaim's mother was very angry. She said Yossi is just overly sensitive and why was my son changed without a discussion? I told her that I will switch her son back, but at the first issue, I would ship him out. She was okay with that. But Yossi's mother is now up in arms. She says, her sons have been loyal campers for ten years, why does a boy get to come and terrorize her son? Can you see a way out of this?

A Going all the way back over literally forty years, I never allowed a person to say, "I don't want a certain kid in my bunk or a certain kid in my class." If you don't like that child, you have every right to go to another bunk. It's too late now to change what you already did, but if it was my call, I would tell Yossi's mother, "If you don't want the other boy with your son, you can take your son out of the bunk," but at the same time I would assure her that I would take good care to make sure all goes well. End of story.

And don't get aggravated over it. No one has a right to dictate anything about other kids no matter what the history.

Unhappy in New School

Q We have a twelve-year-old daughter in the sixth grade. Her school closed down suddenly two summers ago. It was a warm, loving, happy place. We had known for a *while that the school was going through a rough patch, but were guided by our Rav to keep our daughter there because she was content, popular, learning well and loved her principal — all extremely valuable tools for her growth.*

Once the school closed, all the girls were forced to find other schools. The only school that accepted our daughter was one that is considered somewhat liberal in our circles, but we did feel that the academic level would match her needs.

Two years later, she still mourns her old school. She cries often and goes to school with anxiety and apprehension. She is not an overly dramatic child; however, she has said numerous times that she will remember these years as the worst in her life. We spoke with a guidance counselor, and she told us how to help her with anxiety. She has healthy outlets like rollerblading and reading. We validate her feelings, yet simultaneously encourage her to change her thought patterns and try to think positively. Despite the teacher's reports of how well-liked she is, she complains about how immature, thoughtless, and mean the other girls are.

She gets together with her old friends who are part of a new school to which she is begging us to allow her to go. What she doesn't know is that the parents in this new school are seeking to leave. They relayed to us that the school is very weak. At this point, we know we can definitely not reunite her with her old friends in the new school. Also, we intuitively don't think changing schools again is the answer. We know she's in pain and it's hard to watch, but we try to teach her, on her level, that with pain comes growth, and when we make it through difficult times and challenges, we come out stronger.

Are we expecting too much from a twelve-year-old?

And are we correct that changing schools would not make things better, it may even make things worse? Right now, we would not say she is struggling with Yiddishkeit. To us, she's a typical "tween"ager. She does like wearing short socks and her skirts sometimes only just cover her knees. She "hates" Jewish music. I have a couple of teenagers, so these behaviors don't ruffle my feathers. She is young and needs time to understand the beauty of Yiddishkeit and tznius. The question is, how do we navigate her intense dislike and unhappiness?

A First of all, I am very impressed with you as parents. Everything you write is thought out and makes a lot of sense.

I don't think there is anything wrong with telling your daughter that many families are leaving the school she wants to join. But that will not solve the problem.

You are not in an easy position. What may work is hiring a tutor/mentor/big sister for her. This person should be "with it," but frum and *ehrlich*. Officially, she should come to study with your daughter, but her job is to become her best friend. Look for someone really good. Such a person can accomplish more than parents can. She can keep her on the straight and narrow *Yiddishkeit*-wise, and can influence her greatly to become a happier person and stick it out a little while longer. Try this, and please stay in touch.

Progress Report

Q *I hope this email finds you well. This is a long-overdue progress report regarding your eitzah tovah to secure a mentor for our daughter.*

Back in January, the Rav graciously responded to our question regarding our daughter's unhappiness in school.

Two days later, a teacher from her old school reached out to me and asked how she's doing. The timing was incredible and she became her mentor. For two solid months, our daughter's mood changed and it was great! Chasdei Hashem!

After Pesach, she kind of slipped back into her anxious, sad mood. But the summer is an incredible respite for her and does wonders for her self-confidence and spirit.

She's entering seventh grade now. With hope in our hearts and many tefillos on our lips, we daven that she take the good feelings and hold them with her at least for a few months. We will im yirtzeh Hashem try to secure the mentor again.

A I appreciate this email immensely. I must respond to thousands of emails each year, but very few tell me when things go well.

May you have continued *nachas* for many happy and healthy years.

Must We Invite the Entire Class for Shabbos in Our Home?

Q *My ninth-grader wants to invite six other boys to our home for Shabbos. They are all nice boys and they would have a nice Shabbos together. Should I disallow this because other boys might find out and feel bad that they were not part of it?*

A It depends on if these seven boys are close friends. If they are a group that often "hangs out" together and is known to be close, then it is fine. But it is nice of you to have such sensitivity.

In general, there must be ironclad rules in the yeshivah. Our rule for bar mitzvahs generally is as follows: In an average class of twenty-five, you can invite only nine or fewer! From a parallel class, six or fewer.

Once upon a time, many years ago, a *talmid* in our yeshivah had his bar mitzvah in a hotel. He did not plan to invite his entire class. Classes were quite small then, and leaving out only a few boys would be even worse.

Anyway, I walked into that class of the bar mitzvah *bachur*, and I saw two boys sitting there forlornly. I got to the bottom of this story quite quickly. The two boys out of fifteen kids in the class who were not invited were the shleppy kids.

I absolutely hit the roof. I called the father of the bar mitzvah boy. I told him that there is nothing to discuss and that they had until 10:30 in the morning to invite the two kids who were left out. And if not, watch out! The father's response to me was, "But this has nothing to do with the yeshivah." I told him that if by 10:30 those kids weren't invited, their son, the bar mitzvah *bachur*, will be out of yeshivah.

Within a half-hour, the two boys were invited and *shalom al Yisrael.*

The father was angry. "This is not a yeshivah function and you have no right." I told him that he was right. I cannot control the bar mitzvah, but I can control the yeshivah. And if the two kids weren't invited by 10:30, their son would need to look for a new yeshivah.

The two boys went and had a very wonderful time.

When the Guest Room Is Too Small

Baruch Hashem, I have a few married children and also several children living at home. This is a huge berachah, but gets complicated when the married children want to visit. I have a small guest room that fits a couple and a

baby, but not more than that. Now that my eldest daughter has three children, it has become more difficult. The children are too young to sleep by themselves, but there is no room for them in the guest room. They still wake up often at night, so I hesitate to put them with my teenagers, as I feel it would be unfair to expect them to take care of crying children in the middle of the night. So lately, my husband and I take the grandchildren into our own room.

Two of my teenagers share a bedroom that is very large and has an attached bathroom. It would be more than big enough for my daughter's whole family. But they really hate giving up their room and having others in their space. Should my husband and I continue to have the grandchildren sleep in our room when they come, or should I make my teenagers give up their room?

A The grandparents' bedroom should be sacred. The grandchildren should not sleep there. As for the other rooms, your children must know that the house is yours and you have a right to decide who uses which room. Tell your teenagers to give up their room. It is good for them to stretch a little, and it will be a big *chessed* and *hachnasas orchim*. However, your daughter must make sure her children do not touch your teenagers' belongings, as that would be unfair to them. As much as possible, your teenagers should put their things in an inaccessible place before they move out of the room, but ultimately, it is your daughter's responsibility to watch her children.

As a Widow, I Don't Feel I Fit In

Q *I became an almanah one year ago. How can I maintain a sense of dignity and self-respect when I feel that I don't fit in?*

An *almanah* must realize that she always fits in. She sets her own rules and her own guidelines for life. The fact that you are going ahead with life full-steam, functioning fully, in difficult circumstances, shows that you have all the self-dignity in the world. The question is not if you fit in. The question is if the rest of the world fits into your world. This is true for a divorcee and a single woman as well.

Need to Know

Q *I'm going to camp without most of my classmates. I know I shouldn't keep it a secret that I'm a yasom, but it feels awkward to tell people. How should I handle this?*

A You have to protect your feelings. If you are uncomfortable, you should not have to tell anyone. It is really the job of the camp to inform all those who may need to know, to prevent you from facing unnecessary problems. For example, when there is a time devoted to calling parents, it would be hurtful if a fellow camper would ask you if you are calling your parent. Therefore, your primary caretaker should inform the camp so that your counselors and bunk know without you having to tell them. This way, you don't have to talk about it if you don't want to, but everyone has the information that they need in order to be appropriately sensitive to you.

Attending Events for Orphans

Q *I am a yasom but I have never attended an event for yesomim, though I listen to the hotlines. I am too scared to show up at an event. Should I push myself?*

A	This is called anxiety. There are some people who cannot go into crowds. That kind of anxiety is called agoraphobia. Those who fear being in closed spaces have claustrophobia. There are many phobias. Another example would be fear of heights. I suffer from that. The only way to handle it is to fight it. People who fear bridges are instructed to go on a bridge and even stop on it for a few minutes. The more you do what you don't like, the faster you will overcome the fear.

Some people fear davening for the *amud*. When they push themselves to do it anyway, they overcome it. I know a gentleman who was afraid to be called up to the Torah for an *aliyah* for fear of doing something wrong. Since he never tried it, he died never having overcome the fear.

Your phobia is going to the events for *yesomim*. Though you may be uncomfortable the first few times, the only way to overcome it is to attend. Do it a few times and you will be okay. Yes, you should push yourself! You will be fine.

Davening at Home on Yamim Noraim

Q	*I'd like to daven at home over Rosh Hashanah and Yom Kippur. I feel that I'll be able to express my feelings openly and emotionally when I'm not being watched. But I know that tefillah b'tzibbur is an important thing. How can I connect to Hashem through my davening at home, or how can I daven in shul (where I don't feel comfortable crying) and still be the real me?*

A	There is nothing wrong with a girl davening at home and crying her heart out. If that is what makes you comfortable, then do it. Hashem wants to hear that you're talking to Him, and even wants to hear your crying.

Outlawing Clubhouses

Q There is a sentiment in my housing development to outlaw all clubhouses because of the risk of molestation. However, the children are very "into" them. The Rav here recommended that we add a window. He told me to check with a mechanech if it's necessary to completely do away with them. He feels it's not healthy to take away normal things for kids to do, and it's not a given that issues will arise. What is your opinion?

A The Rav is correct. Except that I would not even insist on a window. Don't let a few unusual and infrequent incidents dictate normalcy. Let the kids have a good time. Building a clubhouse is a very healthy outlet for children. I still remember the clubhouse I built when I was a kid. Don't take away kids' youth.

Fads Will Fade Without a Ban

Q I am concerned about a new fad that has arisen in my son's school called "Circle Cards." I do not fully understand the game, but apparently each card has a value, and the boys flip them against each other in hopes of winning and taking the other boys' cards in victory.

I was a big fan of yo-yos, devil sticks etc. as a kid and hated when they were banned; however, now I can see it from a parent's perspective. My son's entire focus has been toward these cards. I hear stories of boys stealing cards, cheating or lying to win more cards, and reluctance to go out and play for fear of missing more "flipping" time. My son's mood when he comes home is a daily reflection of how he fared in the day's flipping games.

My son loves to learn, loves his rebbi, and loves his time in yeshivah. However, I am concerned that this Circle Card fad is turning into legal gambling for children and encouraging all the negative traits (lying, cheating, stealing, etc.) that come along with it.

I'm curious as to your perspective. Should these cards be banned from schools?

A You and many other parents have called and written about this problem. Some of these people are ready to send their children to Gamblers Anonymous! Let's all relax and take a deep breath.

While I understand your concern, I do not believe in banning. When I was a kid in Torah Vodaas, we also flipped cards and did all the same things you describe kids doing today. The difference was, we flipped Mickey Mantle and Willy Mays. I once lost a Mickey Mantle card in flipping! I survived. Our *menahalim* did not ban it. Like all fads, this one will pass. I would not worry about kids becoming gamblers or *ganavim* from it.

Appropriate Reading for Teens

Q *Our daughter is thirteen and enjoys reading. We provide her with lots of books, take her to the library when we can, and purchase the weekly frum children's and teen magazines.*

Our concern is that she also reads the magazines intended for adults as well. She reads them cover to cover. We feel that there are articles in there that are not appropriate for her age. We have gently (and maybe not so gently) informed her what we feel is not appropriate for her to read. However, understandably, that just makes her want to do it more. Is our only option now not to bring it into the house at all?

A This is a very big problem and there are many who are worried about this. I agree with you one hundred percent. When I was a kid, it was even worse, as children read McCall's, Ladies Home Journal, Good Housekeeping, Reader's Digest, and other secular periodicals. The yeshivish thing today is to criticize all the Jewish periodicals, including the *Yated Ne'eman*, *Hamodia*, *Mishpacha*, and *Ami*. Personally, I couldn't disagree more with those who condemn these frum publications. We are forgetting what the dearth of Jewish periodicals meant to previous generations. Boys and girls would go to the local candy store to steal peeks at forbidden things. Teenagers would sit in their local branch of the public library, reading what they shouldn't be reading!

When the decision was made to create the *Yated Ne'eman* in Eretz Yisrael, the editors went to see the Steipler Gaon for his blessings. They told him that they would be putting in *divrei Torah*. He urged them to always remember to publish the news, and that was the purpose of the paper; giving people the news in an *ehrlich* Yiddish paper.

I know the subject matter today is scarier, but if your daughter is going to read anyway, it may as well be these magazines that treat each subject with a Torah approach.

If you are still opposed to her reading them, I don't see any option other than not having them in your home. But even then, she may read them elsewhere. Personally, if it were my daughter, I would prefer she read under my auspices.

Biking During Corona Pandemic

Q *Our fifteen-year-old daughter's friends have invited her to go biking. Due to Coronavirus, the girls need to get out and socialize and get fresh air and exercise. They will all be dressed in a tzniusdig fashion. Is there any general issue with teenaged girls biking in public? Is there a difference between a busy public park and a quiet trail?*

A Biking is a healthy outlet. They should be sure to dress *tzniusdig* and ride only in less-populated areas such as park roads and trails.

Just Football

Q *What is Rabbi Bender's opinion of bachurim watching the Super Bowl?*

A It is a big *b'dieved*. It depends where you live and who his friends are. In communities where everyone is watching, and your son is demanding to watch it, you cannot make your son be the only one left out, especially since he will probably find his own way there and then lie about it. But the obvious conditions must be no commercials and NO HALF-TIME SHOW! And you must find a way to make sure the conditions will be followed, probably by having a responsible person present.

Filter That iPhone

Q *I have a daughter in ninth grade. Baruch Hashem, we are happy with her school and with the chinuch and hashkafos they impart. However, we are a bit dismayed at the widespread ownership of technological devices among the students. It seems that most of her classmates own an iPhone with a strong filter that the school approved. My daughter has been asking for one and feels out of place with her friends by not having one. Baruch Hashem, we have a good relationship with her and trust her and she understands that it would need filters and rules. We really would prefer not to capitulate on this now, but I wonder if it is unfair to her when 80% of her friends have one.*

A This is a tremendous problem today. Many high school students have smartphones. In your community, clearly, nearly all of them own a smartphone. I don't think you can fight it. However, make sure that the phone is fully filtered. You don't want her on social media or sites that can hurt her, *chas veshalom*.

Please Turn Off the Set

Q *We recently moved to a new neighborhood and we're baruch Hashem very happy here and acclimating well. Our neighbors are very welcoming. Our children became very friendly with the neighbors and spend many hours a day playing with them. They are warm, welcoming, great people who do a lot of chessed and hachnasas orchim. They happen to also be a bit more modern than us.*

It has happened once or twice that our five-year-old and three-year-old came home from a neighbor's house and mentioned that they watched Mickey Mouse or other shows of that ilk.

We are wondering how to tackle this issue. Do we make it clear to our son that we expect him not to watch such shows? Do we ignore the issue? Or do we bring the other parents' attention to the fact that we are not comfortable with it?

A I would not worry about Mickey Mouse, but there are certainly things about which you do have to worry. If you don't want even Mickey Mouse, make it clear to your children that your standards are different. There is nothing wrong with telling them that. However, your children are very young. You should offer a strong incentive for walking away/coming home if the neighbors start to watch videos, as they are a powerful draw. You can also ask your neighbor to send your kids home if her family starts a video. Most of the time, rather than sending your son home, they'll wind up not watching the video. If you see that it becomes a problem, write me again.

Zooming With Grandparents During Lockdown

Q *Is it okay to Zoom with grandparents who are stuck at home? The yeshivah has said that they do not allow any Zooming at all. What does the parent tell the child?*

A Grandparents should not be included in the Zoom restriction and you should get the school's permission to Zoom only for this. With the advent of radio, someone came and told the Chofetz Chaim *zt"l* about it. After they explained to him about different channels, the *velt* says that the Chofetz Chaim responded that one day the radio will be used for Torah learning. Different channels or stations would be used for different *masechtos*, etc.

Everything is on Zoom today, and grandparents are locked up at home. It seems that most of the world Skypes today; Zoom is a similar thing. There is no better reason to use Zoom than for this. Yet, if the yeshivah *assurs* it, you cannot do it unless you get *reshus*. If you cannot get through to the yeshivah, then, off the record, you can Zoom and explain to your child that the school didn't mean to forbid using Zoom for communicating with grandparents.

Class Split and He Misses His Friends

Q My rebbi advised me to reach out to the Rosh Yeshivah about my son. My oldest son had an amazing year last year. He is now in second grade. Bli ayin hara, he is one of the better boys in his class. Socially, he did really well last year. He has an amazing circle of friends. Baruch Hashem, he gravitated to the more eidel, mature, geshmak'e boys. We feel that a big part of his growth academically and in ruchniyus was due to his amazing circle of friends.

Yesterday was his first day of school. He was very excited to go back. We were looking forward to his return and to see him come home with the same geshmak as last year. However, when he arrived home, we were pained by his facial expression. He told us that all of his main friends are in the other class. They decided to split last year's class. His chevrah, aside from one boy, are in the other class. This morning, my son asked my wife how many days of school are left this year because he really is very sad about his class. (This has nothing to do with the new rebbi. On the contrary, he's a phenomenal rebbi.) Should we put pressure to have him switched? We spoke to the menahel yesterday, and it didn't seem like there was an option to switch. We are asking the Rosh Yeshivah for guidance in how we should deal with this situation.

A I am surprised that this happened. Normally, schools ask kids to pick friends in the spring, and they guarantee two or three of them. That you were not asked is a *chiddush*. Nevertheless, kids are resilient. If you are *mechazek* him and give him encouragement and some incentives, your son may forget about it in two days. I would not give the same answer in middle school.

At that age, kids are much less forgiving. But for a second-grader, it should be fine.

However, you have every right to try to have your son changed. Schools have their reasons as to why they split classes. But they must understand that parents may and are even obligated to advocate for their child.

Out of the "In-Crowd"

Q My son is in sixth grade. He is extremely bright and mature for his years. However, he has always been extremely sensitive, both physically and emotionally.

Socially, he has friends, but he is not part of the "in-group" in the class. This hurts him very much; however, because of the intellectual/maturity difference between them, their interests are different from his.

Recently, the "in-group" decided they were going to go collecting together on Purim. Only after they made a class announcement that whoever wanted could join did they ask my son if he wanted to join. This brought home to him again that he is not part of that group, and he declined to join them.

Should I try to find a way for him to be a leader and become socially more popular (by, for example, having him arrange for a small group of boys to learn shemiras halashon during breakfast break or the like), or should I allow this to be a place where he develops his "tolerance muscle"?

A As a parent, you cannot do much. When parents try to get involved directly in things like this, it usually does not work. Your son requires counseling with a therapist who specializes in self-esteem and social skills. This process should probably have started years ago, so arrange this as soon as you can, and find someone reputable. But it is certainly fine if a child is different. There is nothing wrong with being a loner, so long as that's what makes the child comfortable. But that doesn't seem to be the case here. A therapist here can be helpful.

Handing Out Treats on Halloween

Q We live in an area where there are many non-Jews and they often knock on our door when going "trick-or-treating." Should I leave a bucket of candy outside my house, or should I open the door and give out the candy, even though my kids will see?

A Rav Pam told everyone to open their doors and treat the kids nicely. You will not go wrong if you do that. And the neighbors on the block loved Rav Pam and his Rebbetzin.

I heard from a parent in our school that she grew up in a city in New Jersey where all her neighbors were non-Jews. She and her siblings got a kick out of seeing the neighbors dressed up, and always gave a small treat to children who came trick-or-treating to their home. None of her siblings went off the *derech* from it.

Will Helping His Friend Put My Son at Risk?

Q My son is in eleventh grade. Several of his friends have gone off the derech. He wants to know, how can he help them without harming himself? How does he hold his ground?

A It depends greatly on how strong your son is. If he is strong, it will only strengthen him to be close to these boys and help them get out of trouble. If his intention is *l'sheim Shamayim*, he will not be hurt. But the reverse is also true. He will be exposed to things you don't want him to be a part of. If he does not have strength of character, he will be burnt.

If he is strong in his own beliefs, he will be able to hold his ground. Then, he will feel an enormous sense of satisfaction if he can turn a boy around.

A friend can help more than others. If the off-the-*derech* young man sees that his friends really care about him, it can do wonders. And you can observe your son along the way. If you see even a slight weakening in his own commitment, you may have to put a stop to the work he is doing with his friend.

Confront Child About Vaping

Q *This morning we encountered a situation that we are unsure how to handle. Our twelve-year-old son's friend called us to tell us that when he came up to his classroom after davening, he found our son vaping in the classroom. He said our son quickly tossed it out the window when he saw his friend.*

We're just not sure how to deal with this. We don't want him to be angry with his friend, but this is definitely something we need to discuss with him. What should our approach to this be?

A Of course, don't mention the friend. And don't get over-excited. Unfortunately, vaping is common in junior high school today. Just sit down with him calmly, and explain why he is not doing a smart thing. It has become a horror for schools. Children believe there is nothing wrong and they know how to hide it very well.

Mussar for Chassanim
to Quell Divorce Rate

Q Is the lack of mussar learning one of the causes of the high divorce rate? If bachurim in mesivta and beis medrash had more structured or mandatory mussar seder, would it help?

A Most of the time, the answer, unfortunately, is no. They will understand nothing until it is *l'maiseh.* I give a *vaad* to our kollel on *shalom bayis.* They are then married and can appreciate the applicable *mussar. Mussar* is very important, but *lav davka* to *bachurim* who have no *shaychus* to it. Somehow, if we talk *mussar* to the *talmidim,* many will not apply it to marriage. Ongoing *vaadim* and *shmuessen* to *chassanim,* however, are urgently needed.

Teenaged Drivers

Q My son had a mesibah at his rebbi's house. My wife and I were unable to drive him. Some of his friends are driving, and my son asked to go with them. I said no, as I am not comfortable with a high-school boy driving with a bunch of other boys in the car. We attempted to arrange a van, which would have been fifteen dollars per person, but none of the other boys were interested. My son missed the mesibah. I am wondering if I did the right thing.

A It is too late to change the past, but I agree with you; I am a terrible worrier when it comes to kids driving. However, the bottom line is kids are getting their licenses early and we have very little control over this. Would I let my son go with a young driver? NO. But I would also make sure to get my kid there, even if I had to drive. I tell parents constantly, you should not give car keys to your child unless he promises not to go even one mile above the speed limit and never takes other kids in the car, as this makes them drive wildly and show off. But I am afraid you and I are in the minority. However, you should have found a way to get your son to his rebbi's home.

The Cholent Chaburah

Q My son is in ninth grade in a local mesivta. Baruch Hashem, he seems to be doing well and also seems happy.

A minhag has arisen here in town where many bachurim go to various eateries on Thursday night to sit around and shmooze and eat cholent and kugel. I understand that the boys need an outlet sometimes, but to me, it does not seem healthy for this to happen every single week. (I also wonder how much good can come out of a group of unsupervised ninth-graders sitting around for long periods of time.) I am not happy for my son to participate.

However, I know that in chinuch one needs to choose his battles. While I work hard to keep my relationship with my son warm, we do sometimes tend to "have it out" with these types of things; he is not someone who is mekabel easily. Is this a battle I should pick?

A This has become a very big thing with *bachurim*. While I don't know how positive it is, you are correct that you must choose your battles. This is a fight you should NOT pick, but I would put limits. Allow him to participate once or twice a month and that's it. Additionally, try to keep an eye on who are his *chevrah*.

Social Drinking Can Be Antisocial

Q Do you classify "social" drinking (e.g., Friday night beer in yeshivah, however small the amount) in the same category as smoking and vaping? And what would be the reason?

A Yes, somewhat. Because like smoking and vaping, drinking can quickly become addictive, especially in those predisposed to it. Both behaviors are dangerous. Unfortunately, this has become a problem in yeshivos and the world at large in a very bad way. This can be found across the entire spectrum of *Yiddishkeit*. We must try harder to obliterate this terrible issue.

Specific Circumstances

Facing Tragedy in School

Q Our community school is one where nearly everyone in the school, both faculty and students, are acquaintances, if not good friends. Recently, we came to school to the news that a teacher's seven-month-old son was in the hospital in critical condition because he had stopped breathing during the night.

The hallways felt like Tishah B'Av. Teachers were pacing with distraught faces; many had obviously just been crying.

During the course of the morning, we learned that the child was niftar.

The grief and sadness on the part of the teachers was so overt that some of my young students asked me, "Did someone die?" and "Why are all the teachers crying?"

My own feeling about how to deal with the situation was very different from the above. I told my class at the beginning of the day that a child in the community was *in a serious situation and we should daven for him. I took the opportunity to drive home the lessons of "count your blessings" and "what is really important in life."*

When we heard the devastating news, I told my class what had happened without telling them the last name. However, I did not openly grieve, and I spoke to my students in the regular way, without any outward display of pain. As terrible as the situation is, I thought that the students are in school and the show must go on.

Of course, I am hurting. This teacher taught my kids. She is good friends with my wife. I just felt that it was wrong for the situation to hijack the operation of the school. What is the correct way to deal with such a situation?

A You are handling it perfectly correctly, but there is nothing wrong with teachers crying. Sometimes I get upset that because I deal with so many issues, I have become hardened and do not react enough. All the reactions are normal and correct. May we only know of *simchos*.

Therapy Needed With Signs of OCD

Q *My son is nineteen years old and is truly a metzuyan in every way. He is a baal middos, a masmid, and a sweet bachur whom everyone likes.*

He is very midakdek on his tefillos, especially his long Shemoneh Esrei. I noticed several years ago that during his long tefillos, he repeated the same words several times. At that time I dismissed it as nothing to worry about.

Recently, on his off Shabbosos, he has been sitting next to me in shul and I can hear him repeating words in Krias Shema and Shemoneh Esrei over and over — even Hashem's Name. I am not sure how to address this.

A This sounds like classic Obsessive-Compulsive Disorder. This will not get better on its own; on the contrary, untreated, it is likely to get much worse. There are many excellent psychologists and therapists who work with this today. It has become a very common problem. Don't wait. Have him see someone immediately.

Including Relative With Disabilities in a Simchah

Q *I have a niece with severe disabilities. She is confined to a wheelchair, is fed by tube, and can't communicate clearly. It's often difficult to include her when we're planning family events, but we do our best to make accommodations so that she can enjoy and feel part of things.*

We have an exciting simchah coming up: my oldest sister's first chasunah. My sister-in-law, my niece's mother, asked me if my teenaged daughters and their cousins could help her feel included in the fun. I asked my two girls to take turns with a couple of other cousins to push her wheelchair, sit with her, include her in the conversations, and make sure she's not left on the sidelines. I know that it means giving up some of their fun in the evening, but I'm surprised and disappointed that they're complaining about having to do this. It's only an hour or so for each of them, and I would have hoped that they could empathize with their cousin who can't join in anything on her own. How can I help them understand this and react with more positivity and willingness to this chessed opportunity?

A It really depends on how old the children are. Young kids are busy with themselves, and it is understood that they don't want to give up their time. But teenagers should understand what it means to help a handicapped child.

We have many children with disabilities in our yeshivah. I always say, the biggest *chessed* is not for those children, but rather for the other students who learn how to take care of and interact with them. I doubt a child in our yeshivah would not run to take a chance to sit with his cousin. It is a school culture, and it should be internalized in the same way in all schools. Who has not been at a wedding of a Chai Lifeline volunteer where the *chassan* is busy dancing with the child who was his camper? That is why we should be encouraging our children to do this kind of work in the summer. It is an ongoing inculcation. Start now! Perhaps a half-hour instead of an hour for each cousin would be plenty of time to cover the evening.

Should Our Teenage Brother Care for Our Disabled Mother?

Q *We have a question about our brother. We are seven married siblings and our brother lives alone with our mother. Our mother was in a severe car accident a few years ago that left her with many limitations. Our brother has been taking care of her, with the help of her aide. The problem is, our brother is only seventeen. We feel he should be learning and attending school like any boy his age. At this point, he often skips minyan and doesn't shtel tzu with the learning in school. We feel like he is using our mother's condition as an excuse. We had an idea to have him move in with a relative so that he will be more regular in his school attendance and less distracted in his learning. What is Rabbi Bender's opinion?*

A I'm sorry to disagree with you, but I think this is a bad idea. The boy is doing a huge *chessed* and tremendous *kibbud eim*. He will not lose out from that. If you send him away from home, you are sending a damaging message. He will feel unwanted and suffer from being away from his mother. Leave him alone. Perhaps you can find him a mentor who will encourage better attendance, but that may also improve on its own as he grows a little older. Of course, you must encourage him to be a regular yeshivah *bachur* — but to send him away? *Chas veshalom!* Perhaps you and your siblings could try to help out by coming more often to attend to your mother so that your brother will be relieved.

On a personal note, I stayed home with my mother for nearly eight years until I was married. It may have been one of the biggest *berachos* of my life. In order to live at home, I traveled the subways morning and night, every single day, rather than sleeping in yeshivah. In retrospect, this was a very tremendous *kinyan* for me.

Stepfather Is Out of Line

Q My mother remarried almost three years ago. My stepfather gets very uncomfortable when we talk about our lives before he was part of it. We are not allowed to talk about any memories of our father. He got pretty upset when I lit a candle and was not in the best mood on the yahrtzeit. This obviously makes my mother uneasy. On one hand, I feel that doing things for the yahrtzeit is kibbud av for my father, but on the other hand, is it a lack of kibbud eim if it upsets my mother because it bothers her husband?

A I believe your stepfather is mistaken. Please find an adult he respects to speak to him. You have every right and even obligation to keep the flame of your father burning, both literally and figuratively.

The most successful second marriages have clear understandings of this issue. The new spouse understands that the first spouse is not disappearing overnight. They even agree to discuss the relevant issues about their deceased spouses. I don't think your stepfather is acting very maturely, but your mother is, so to speak, stuck between a rock and a hard place.

Must Yeshivos Provide Special Ed?

Q Halachically speaking, do Orthodox Jewish day schools serving the heimishe kehillah have a requirement to secure special educational provision called for by a pupil's special educational needs? Is a comment of "Sorry, we'd love to help, but unfortunately, we don't have the resources" or the like valid?

A A major essay is required to fully answer this question. Suffice it to say that it is the achrayus of every rebbi and yeshivah to make sure that every single Jewish child is educated properly. Once a school has accepted a child, it is their job to set up the proper curriculum to serve that child. Yes, the school may have to spend money on certain programs, but most children can be educated.

There are exceptions where there is no way the child can be educated in the yeshivah. That child may need a special school or even the public school system. That is a decision that the school can make after a few years of trying to educate the child.

There are many maamarei Chazal about the responsibility to educate children. See Sanhedrin 91b at the very bottom. "Kol hamonea…" See the Maharsha on this Gemara. There are many other examples.

Will Moving Have a Negative Impact on the Kids?

Q My wife and I have been discussing the idea of moving out of town. There are a lot of benefits for us, such as cheaper housing and tuition. There's also the possibility of getting a new start in a new community, which we feel would benefit us both as a couple. Additionally, my wife is working full time, and we'd like to be able to change that.

We're concerned, though, about how that might affect our kids. We have, bli ayin hara, five children ranging in age from four to thirteen. Does it make sense to uproot kids from familiar surroundings? Is that just a part of building resilience? For our middle child — who's been a bit of a challenge — in particular, we've had excellent support from her current school. Does it make sense to move her in the face of other benefits?

A Generally, those who move out of town for your reasons do not have problems with their kids. Occasionally, children — especially in grades four through six — have a difficult time getting acclimated to new friends. Interestingly enough, as a general rule, children in lower grades have very few issues. Those finishing elementary school often go off to a new yeshivah anyway.

Of course, there is an adjustment period. But remember, when the home is happier, and your wife can be home and not working as many hours, you are already ahead of the game. As far as your middle child, some places out of town do not have the levels of support that New York has, but it really depends on the city. Major cities like Chicago, Houston, Baltimore, and Cleveland may have what you need. Do your homework and choose wisely.

Rigid Rules Must Be Obeyed

Q *My brother is getting married out of town in a few weeks and I booked tickets for my whole family to attend. I asked my son's Rosh Yeshivah if I can have reshus to take my son out of yeshivah for a day and a half to attend the wedding and he said no. I am so angry!*

I paid an extra $500 so that he would miss less yeshivah. I am not asking to take him out for a vacation; I am asking them to allow him to attend his only uncle's wedding. I am not angry about the wasted money. I am angry that he is saying no.

A I wanted to take one of my grandchildren to Eretz Yisrael last year. His yeshivah did not allow it.

I agree with you. I do not understand how a *menahel* does not allow a boy to attend his uncle's wedding. I used to ask Rav Elya Svei these *shailos*; he held family is very important.

I was upset last year; you are upset this year. I would try asking again. If permission is not granted, move on. It is not the end of the world. I learned that I had to accept the school's decision. So must you. It doesn't mean you have to agree, but don't make a fight with the school over it, and definitely don't badmouth the Rosh Yeshivah in your son's presence.

Sharing Coronavirus Updates

Q *Regarding Coronavirus, should we be informing our children of every update?*

A Certainly not. The less news we share, the better. Only when there is news of progress can we share. There are some children who need to know all the info of the time.

The less they know, the better. You cannot lie to them, but you don't have to tell them everything.

Holocaust Narratives Can Be Frightening

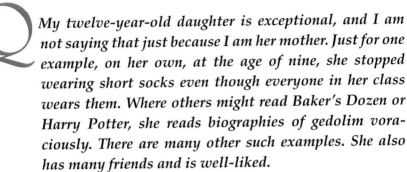

My twelve-year-old daughter is exceptional, and I am not saying that just because I am her mother. Just for one example, on her own, at the age of nine, she stopped wearing short socks even though everyone in her class wears them. Where others might read Baker's Dozen or Harry Potter, she reads biographies of gedolim voraciously. There are many other such examples. She also has many friends and is well-liked.

Though an avid reader, she does not read Holocaust books because she finds them too scary. I thought it was time to encourage that. When I mentioned her fear in passing to her mechaneches, she cornered me with lots of questions and started throwing around labels like anxiety disorder, OCD, etc.

So she finds the Holocaust scary and is an otherwise exceptional child. Does every child who stands out in some way have something wrong with them?

I don't know your daughter, but based on what you are writing, I would disagree vehemently with the *mechaneches*. I know many children who cannot read stories of the Holocaust, even at a much older age. Most of these are very good, serious children who bleed and cry from what they read. That does not mean they have OCD or any type of anxiety disorder! I don't see any OCD with the *frumkeit* she has chosen. Unless there is more to the story that I am not hearing, I see an elevated *neshamah* who has chosen a wonderful way of life. She is popular and well-liked. The only way she can be labeled is if there are other issues you haven't mentioned that are affecting her. Assuming those don't exist, Hashem should *bentch* you with many more children like this.

Holocaust Reading Too Frightening for Young Children

Q *Our oldest child is almost six years old and very smart, baruch Hashem. With Tishah B'Av coming up, I was wondering if it is appropriate to tell him or read him stories about the Holocaust. We want our children to be happy kids with a positive outlook on Yiddishkeit. I've heard that some chinuch experts say not to let children read stories about the Holocaust because it can give them questions about emunah.*

A I would not read children Holocaust stories, certainly not at bedtime. They are much too horrific for children of such a young age. I remember many years ago when my son was ten years old, he read the first major book of Holocaust stories by Yaffa Eliach. He woke up in the middle of the night screaming from a nightmare.

I would not give Holocaust books to children under bar mitzvah. It is fine for them to hear stories from speakers who will speak without details. However, stories about the *Churban* are fine. All children growing up in a Torah environment hear stories about the *Churban* constantly. We finish every *Shemoneh Esrei* with the *tefillah* that Hashem should rebuild the Beis HaMikdash quickly. Therefore, it is fine to tell stories of the *Churban* to young children, just without the horrific stories detailed in *Maseches Gittin*.

Taking Children to an Unveiling

Q We will soon be traveling out of town for my wife's grandfather's hakamas matzeivah. We wanted to know if it would be wise and/or appropriate to bring our children. Our oldest, though only five, has been asking for months where Zeidy's body and neshamah are. Our three-year-old talks about Zeidy a lot too, but only asks when she will see him again and when Mashiach is coming. Our baby is named for this Zeidy and we feel like it might bring nechamah to people if he is there.

A You may definitely bring all the children. It will only affect the five-year-old, and that in a positive way. Perhaps it may bring her some closure.

Bonding Time Is Essential

Q My son is having a difficult time in yeshivah this year. In order to help motivate him, I offered that, if over the next four weeks he would show that he is putting effort into his learning, as a reward, I would take him on a hike after yeshivah on Sunday, just him and me.

He was very excited about it. However, he has been asking if he can spend the entire day with me as the reward and skip yeshivah on Sunday.

My wife and I are a little nervous to agree to this, especially as he missed part of the school day last Sunday because of a family simchah.

A It is absolutely fine to take your son out of yeshivah for bonding time with his father. Nothing is more important in a boy's development than his relationship with his father. As long as this is not done too often, it is perfectly fine.

What's in a Name?

Q My father remarried and everyone expects me to accept his new wife as my mother. I respect her and we get along okay, but one thing I can't do is call her Mommy or anything resembling that. What do I do?

A *Baruch Hashem,* you get along with your new mother. Continue to work on it.

This is a very difficult question to answer. There are three parts here. Your father's feelings, his new wife's feelings, and your own feelings. Right now, your father is trying to make his marriage work, and that will be to your benefit also. One day, you will get married and be out of the house and it will be good for you that your father has a wife. Also, if your new stepmother is not happy, she can make your father miserable, which will NOT be good for you.

However, I understand your feelings very well. No one can or ever will replace your mother. Therefore, you should compromise. Since you called your mother Mommy, call your stepmother Ima or something of that nature. Others have called their stepmothers by their first names. There are many opinions here.

But there is something else that is very important. You may have younger siblings who need a mommy and may have never known their birth mother. They must call your stepmother *Mommy* because she is raising them. It would be very awkward if you did not call her by the same name your younger siblings do.

Babysitter Used Phone Inappropriately

Q We had someone babysit for us recently, and we left my wife's phone at home so she could contact us because she did not have her own phone. Today, my wife was looking *through her search history, and she came across very inappropriate searches that were not her own. Do we have a responsibility to tell the girl's parents? Are we to blame for leaving the phone with her?*

You should never leave such a phone with a teenager. If you do, this kind of thing is almost certain to happen. However, you should not tell the parents. Perhaps this was a one-time occurrence. Nor should you feel guilty. That accomplishes nothing — just resolve never to do that again.

Separate Swimming at Ten Years Old

I am wondering if it's permissible for my ten-year-old son to go swimming along with a fifteen-year-old girl who is wearing a tznius cover-up.

Is it a halachic issue? Hashkafic? Both?

My instinct is that it's not okay and I haven't permitted it. However, I would like to learn and understand what the issue is.

It is not the right thing. Ten-year-old kids know a lot already in this day and age. Even those rabbanim who are lenient with ages in these issues agree that it should not be past the age of seven.

The Best Seats in the House

The Siyum HaShas is coming up soon, and I want to make it as exciting as possible for my entire family, including my married children. I've rented hotel rooms near the siyum so we can go early and eat like mentchen, and after the siyum, not have to wait in traffic for hours.

I even rented a van to take us all to the hotel, then to the siyum, then back to the hotel, all for kavod haTorah.

Now I am deciding which tickets to get. There are cheap "nosebleed" seats, more expensive seats near the dais with a clear view of all the chashuve Rabbanim, and even more expensive seats in a warm area with food service.

Where do I sit my family? In comfort, with food, or in the cold? In the suite with warmth and food is spoiling them, but then again, so is going to a hotel. But they will enjoy the six-hour event a lot more. Or on the field with a view of the true heroes of the siyum, but in the cold where they might complain for six hours?

A It is in January. Obviously, if it will be freezing cold, we will all have a problem. Assuming the weather is tolerable, facing the Rabbanim and being part of the crowd is preferable. You want the kids to be part of the *avirah*, to feel the pride that they are part of this great nation. The suites do not bring out the best in the event. They become all about the food, running around, etc. The seats on the field are the way to go.

Be Careful With Karate

Q *We wanted the Rosh Yeshivah's opinion on having a karate class on Sundays in our home for a few five-year-olds. The teacher is a frum Yid. These are kids who need strengthening in coordination and balance. The goal would not be to become a fighter, but rather to strengthen their bodies with this form of exercise.*

A Ordinarily, I do not believe in taking lessons in martial arts. I feel, and I am not alone, that kids who are busy learning self-defense often end up becoming physically aggressive. I know that this response will not be popular with people in this field, one man's opinion. But here, there is an overriding reason for these particular children, so in this case, for a reason like this, it is fine.

I do feel it is important to research the karate teacher. Anytime an adult is working in close contact with a child, you want to be sure that there are no issues in private areas with the instructor. I was never comfortable with Boy Scouts. I remember many years ago when a group of people in our community wanted to open a new Boy Scout troop. I was vehemently opposed. While I am sure these particular instructors were fine people, Chazal do teach us, "*kabdeihu v'chashdeihu* — honor him but remain suspicious of him." We must be careful when a 58-year-old person wants to take children on an overnight hike. Why would any 58-year-old want to sleep in the forest with mosquitoes without facilities? Therefore, again, whenever adults get involved with children, be it choirs, scouting, karate, private tutoring, etc. we must do our due diligence.

Watching Kosher Videos

Q *Considering the difficulty of having everyone home 24/7, can a family who ordinarily does not use technology at all for entertainment show kosher videos to their children?*

A They should not do it. They should follow their *derech hachaim*. And yes, it falls on the mothers' shoulders. If a family already watches videos, then it is okay to watch a little more. Parents have asked me how to prevent children from getting interested in sports. It is impossible to avoid completely; just set time limits.

Watching Sports at Home

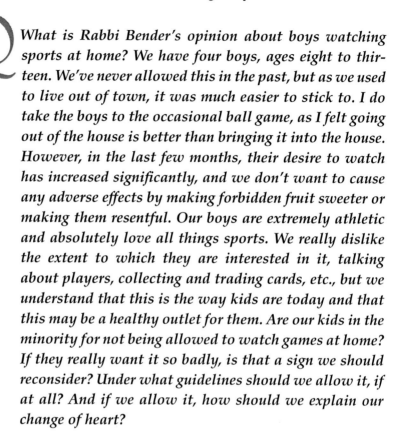

Q What is Rabbi Bender's opinion about boys watching sports at home? We have four boys, ages eight to thirteen. We've never allowed this in the past, but as we used to live out of town, it was much easier to stick to. I do take the boys to the occasional ball game, as I felt going out of the house is better than bringing it into the house. However, in the last few months, their desire to watch has increased significantly, and we don't want to cause any adverse effects by making forbidden fruit sweeter or making them resentful. Our boys are extremely athletic and absolutely love all things sports. We really dislike the extent to which they are interested in it, talking about players, collecting and trading cards, etc., but we understand that this is the way kids are today and that this may be a healthy outlet for them. Are our kids in the minority for not being allowed to watch games at home? If they really want it so badly, is that a sign we should reconsider? Under what guidelines should we allow it, if at all? And if we allow it, how should we explain our change of heart?

A It is clear that you have a device in your home, either a television or a computer, that enables the kids to watch ball games. I am not sure why you allow that. We should never, ever allow a TV into our homes. Forgive me, but having a TV is almost like having a bathroom in the middle of your living room. You clearly want to raise *bnei Torah*. You were happy that when you lived out of town, this wasn't an issue. Now, you chose where to live and have created an issue. Now that you have set this as your standard, as you also seem to realize, you cannot *assur* everything. You must meet them in the middle. I would recommend allowing watching on Sundays only. You can explain that, although not your first choice, you realize how much this means to them and you don't want them to be miserable.

It would be if they didn't watch in your own home. Let them go elsewhere — to a friend you trust or a grandparent — for an hour a week. Keep your home *kadosh*.

As far as explaining it to the kids, there is nothing wrong with saying you made a big mistake. *Hatzlachah* on your new venture. It is not easy to take away something the kids are already used to, but you are doing the correct thing.

Don't Sweat the Sweatpants

Q *My eight-year-old son has been asking me frequently if we can get him sweatpants for playing. Many of his neighbors and cousins have them.*

On the one hand, he just wants to copy the others, as he perceives this as "cool" or "in."

On the other hand, we are not into this casual, almost goyish look.

We are wondering if we should just get them for him, or use this opportunity to teach him that not everything that everyone does is something we should copy.

A This really depends on how prominent this type of dress is among his peers. If most of the other kids wear them, allow him to as well. Pick your battles. It is quite common, even in the finest schools and communities, that children who are eight years old wear sweatpants. Of course, don't do it if the school has a suggested dress code, even if it's not compulsory.

Sharing the Yated

Q I have a question about what comes first, hakaras hatov, or being mezakeh the tzibbur? I get the Yated Ne'eman every week in yeshivah and only read it for a few minutes on Thursday night, after which I give it away. Should I give it to my chavrusa, a yungerman to whom I have tremendous hakaras hatov, even though only he and his wife will enjoy it? Or do I leave it in the yeshivah dorm and then all the bachurim can enjoy it?

A This is a beautiful question. You should give it to your chavrusa. Hakaras hatov comes first. A kollel yungerman is likely not financially well-to-do and will appreciate it very much. And his wife can enjoy it too.

Employee Loyalty Is Expected

Q I have a slight disagreement with a colleague regarding the dedication that an employee in a yeshivah should have toward his employer.

Our school has a kindergarten rebbi who has been here for nearly two decades. Recently, we brought in a UPK program that admittedly placed a strain on the rebbi, as it includes outside scrutiny, periodic visits, and routines to which he was not accustomed, etc. But it is a tremendous source of income for our struggling mossad.

On the plus side, this has brought him (1) a full-time assistant, (2) a maximum of eighteen kids in the class where he used to have up to thirty, (3) a beautifully furnished classroom, and unlimited supplies. This mossad also pays significantly more than comparable mosdos in our area, so he is very fortunate to have this job.

Once in a blue moon, the rebbi is called upon to do something outside yeshivah hours. For example, an inspector was running late and would come past dismissal time. He complained that waiting would make him late for his English teaching job, for which he will be fined $60. He said he would not wait unless compensated (though he has no problem with regularly coming fifteen to twenty minutes late).

Now, I sympathize with the loss of money and with the feeling of being cornered. But I thought this was a bit much, considering all the rebbi gains from his employment here.

A I think rebbeim must understand that things change and they must be flexible, especially when he is doing better than his peers financially. Sometimes employees forget that employers do expect loyalty. I know that I consider it a prerequisite before we hire a new employee.

My wife became a high school teacher shortly after we were married. She went to work for the world-renowned *gadol* in *chinuch* and Torah, Harav Manis Mandel *shlita*. She came home from her erev school faculty meeting a bit disappointed. Rav Mandel spoke for a very long time about loyalty to one's school. She had expected *chinuch* tips and ideas from this great *manhig*. Recently, she reminded me of that day more than forty years ago. "Now, after all these years in *chinuch*, I understand what Rav Mandel meant and understood. Rebbeim and moros need to know that by kvetching and forever complaining, they can literally ruin the school. We need to once in a while turn around and appreciate our working conditions. I do feel the school should reimburse a rebbi for any time he misses because of a school issue. But staff should appreciate their employers, even if it means changing one's style sometimes or even the hours. That is what education is all about. There will be change and we must adapt.

Diverting Parents From School Camp

Q Every year, our school runs a camp that brings in much-needed income. This year, a morah in our preschool who is also a parent decided to open her own camp. She is targeting our parents, cutting deals with them, etc. The parents initially assume that she's reaching out for the school's camp. The camp director is livid. Our school's dean is concerned. Do we threaten to not have her return as a morah?

A Our yeshivah runs a day camp. The rebbeim all understand that if they are offered a job elsewhere, they must ask us before accepting. We never had such a situation of a morah or rebbi helping the competition. I cannot tell you what to do, but if this were one of our moros, I would call her in and tell her to desist immediately or look for a new job.

Sneaking Snacks

Q Our six-year-old daughter is a very smart and independent girl. We try to encourage her independence and strength of character. However, we do run into some issues. Since she was two years old, she has been helping herself to food when she wants it. Recently, it has become mostly snacks and nosh. Instead of forbidding, we try to teach her to fill her body with healthy food and save the nosh for later. However, this has led instead to her taking nosh (no matter where it's hidden) and hiding it among her stuff. When asked, she will lie about it and claim she has no idea. We don't want to make this a fight, but we also don't want her to have whatever, whenever. We don't want her to think lying is an acceptable way to get whatever she wants.

When approached about anything, even in a non-confron-tational way, her response is extreme. She explodes and feels very misunderstood. How do we find the proper bal-ance? The issue is not just a food issue. Her sisters some-times come home with a toy from gan and it can disappear for two or three days, then show up in her knapsack with her claiming, "I got it from a friend."

A   I once heard a nutritionist and eating disorder specialist say, "If a kid is stealing a tuna sandwich, he's hungry. If he's stealing a sour stick, his parents are health nuts." Fact: kids love nosh. Many will do anything to get some. Your daughter is hardly the only child to take forbidden nosh when parents aren't looking. Some parents put locks on the pantry and fridge. That is certainly an option. But don't expect a six-year-old to stop sneaking nosh. I do believe that if you wouldn't be so tough against nosh, the other problems wouldn't develop. Don't forget, she is only six years old. Zeidies and Bubbies sneak nosh when their kids aren't looking!

If the lying gets more serious, let me know. I may have some ideas.

Censoring Difficult Issues in the Parashah

Q   *I've been teaching parashah to my class of three- and four-year-olds for about twenty years. This past week, I was approached by the director of my daycare regarding my parashah newsletter. She explained that the new approach is to teach only the positive/good points in the parashah, not the stories of punishment or anything of that nature. In fact, no parshiyos past Tetzaveh should be taught. Is this the correct way? If yes, can you please explain so I can work on changing my mindset and do what is best for future doros?*

This is absolutely not our *derech*. I have never heard of a child being traumatized by stories from the *parashah* and see no reason to adopt this practice. However, it is not a big enough *avlah* to make a fuss over. While you are in this school, you should follow their directives.

Absent While Present

I have something that I want to discuss with my daughter's school and I want to ask if my thinking is correct.

For seventh grade through high school, the school has a policy that if a girl is seen talking during davening, or if she's more than five minutes late, she's marked as "absent." I am totally fine with strict rules relating to tefillah to teach the children to value and respect it, but the way they are doing it is against the simple, basic principles of good chinuch.

The message the school is teaching the girls is that sheker for a good purpose is fine. The girl is "present," not "absent." She may be late, or if she's talking (or not davening) she is not fully participating, but she is 100% present and not "absent." In fact, once she's marked absent by the teacher, she's still not allowed to leave school for that period. So she's officially absent and yet being forced to be present at the same time. An incomprehensible contradiction.

(Last year, once she was marked as absent, she was allowed to leave the davening room. Once she was allowed to leave, she didn't daven at all. So in the name of being strict about davening rules, they allowed my daughter to not daven at all. Missing the forest for the trees. This year, in her new division, I think they make them daven in a different room, so maybe that issue has been corrected, but that still means they are not absent.)

In my opinion, this system is undeniably sheker. They are teaching our kids that it's okay to twist, distort, and even redefine words and concepts if it fits one's desired goals. This is an avlah even if the goals are noble. When they get older, they will remember this lesson and do the same. It's school-sponsored terrible chinuch.

I think the school has every right to be strict, but they need to change their system to have a mark of "inadequate participation," which can include lateness, talking, disrupting, or simply not davening.

When I spoke with an administrator there last year, the person really didn't understand what I was saying, and justified their policy by saying, "Other schools do it, too."

What are the Rosh Yeshivah's thoughts?

A Far be it from me to give opinions about girls' schools, But I will try to answer to the best of my ability.

First, there is a major argument in girls' schools about how to respond when students are five minutes late and not admitted to davening. For those who have a supervised side room for them, it may not be so bad. In the boys' yeshivah, if the boys are five minutes late, we thank them for coming.

But with girls, the streets of our community are in total chaos from 8:20-8:30 a.m. Girls are running through the streets to get to school on time. I am not in their cars, but in the cars, the girls must be screaming to parents, "Get me there on time! Please!" because there is more honking in those ten minutes than there is in the rest of the day put together.

So, I will not say yes or no to the policy. But to mark a child absent, when she is not, does not seem to be *yashrus*. Perhaps go over the policy with them, to find out the other side of the story.

But to me it seems wrong. Also, we should not forget that we want to see our children daven in a *mentchlich* manner, so if they are late, let's give them the opportunity to daven nicely, under supervision.

When Something Is Amiss ...

Saving the Child Is Imperative

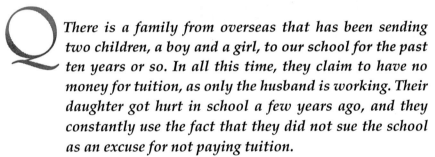 There is a family from overseas that has been sending two children, a boy and a girl, to our school for the past ten years or so. In all this time, they claim to have no money for tuition, as only the husband is working. Their daughter got hurt in school a few years ago, and they constantly use the fact that they did not sue the school as an excuse for not paying tuition.

At this point, the boy, an eighth-grader, is unfortunately not frum and is barely coming to yeshivah. He only does so as a favor to his parents (who are frum to an extent), but he is begging them to switch him to public school.

I have kept him in school because I simply have rachmanus and don't want this child to be lost to a public school education. At this point, however, the parents have not paid a penny and are seriously considering switching the children to public school.

The board is asking me what I think should be done

and I told them it is something for daas Torah to decide. They want to tell the family to keep the kids home until they reach a decision, but I think that will just push them into public school sooner. What does the Rosh Yeshivah advise?

A You must continue to try to save the boy. I understand the sentiment of the board, but a child's *neshamah* is at stake. Financial considerations cannot be permitted to override that.

Dealing With Anxiety in Sleepaway Camp

Q *My son is currently in eighth grade. He has struggled for some time with low self-esteem and anxiety. World events this past year, between Covid-19, riots in New York City, and what happened in Meron, have taken a significant toll, and his anxiety level has reached a new high.*

Although he is now seeing someone once a week to help with this anxiety, he is unable to go to sleep at night unless either my wife or I stay with him. He has begun to take light medication to aid him in falling asleep.

My son is currently scheduled to go to a three-week sleepaway camp for the first time. Our neighbor runs the camp and another neighbor is a learning rebbi there. Still, I am very nervous about sending him. On top of everything else, he is a very sensitive boy, almost to a fault.

A The best thing you can do for your son is to send him to sleepaway camp. Try to find an older counselor or yungerman in camp who can watch over him and speak to him whenever he feels he is experiencing anxiety. Try to find out the name of his counselor beforehand and be in touch with him. Anxiety has become very common in the past couple of years; it is something we deal with daily. Don't let your anxiety about your son's situation get in the way of your son making it. Don't call the camp during those weeks! Leave them to do their jobs.

It also goes without saying that a good therapist is critical!

Hatzlachah rabbah.

Neighbor's Child Frightens Our Children

Q *I have a neighbor who is very chutzpadig and does not respect authority. It's come to the point where my kids are scared when he comes to our yard, and I can't let them out unless I am there with them to quash any verbal abuse and to make sure no damage is done to our yard toys. I've spoken to the boy's father once, but that doesn't seem to have been effective. What can I do?*

A This is a very difficult situation. Do whatever you have to do. If the child is hurting your children, you must separate them. One of the hardest issues is dealing with a neighbor's child. There is a reluctance to get involved with a neighbor because of how important it is to get along with one's neighbor. And that is very well understood.

The only real *eitzah* is to sit down with the softer of the two parents — the one who will listen well without getting excited — and talk over the situation. Explain that while you understand the concept that kids will be kids, you would like to work together with your neighbors to ensure that the children play nicely. Don't be accusatory; present a "let's do something together" attitude. If done with purity and a good heart, you will *iy"H* be successful.

Sadness Is a Natural Emotion

Q *I know it is a mitzvah to be "b'simchah tamid — constantly happy." Is it ever okay to be sad?*

A It is perfectly fine to be sad. In fact, some people actually enjoy being sad. They are happiest when they are miserable. But everyone feels sad sometimes. Many cry and they feel relieved when they cry. Sadness is an emotion like any other; it is part and parcel of our make-up. What we must watch out for is too much of feeling sorry for ourselves. When that happens, we cannot accomplish what we must because we are too busy wallowing in our grief. That can be very unhealthy.

Horrified by Browsing History

Q *My son has been sliding, both academically and in his behavior. He has stopped going to minyan for Minchah and comes late to Shacharis. He is not putting in effort in school and has begun acting out as well.*

He has acquired a smartphone, which he uses incessantly behind our backs. Recently, I had access to his phone and checked his browsing history. Suffice it to say that there were things there that are poison for a Yiddishe neshamah. Should I confront him? Will he feel betrayed because I checked his phone? I feel like he is throwing his life away. Shouldn't I, as his parent, tell him that? Explain to him where he is headed?

A Your son is at risk and you must seek help for him. But don't ever let him know that you know what is on his cell phone. You will lose him completely. He will absolutely feel betrayed. You must keep your relationship positive in any way you can. He knows very well how you would feel about what he is doing and where he is headed. He is struggling and you must get him help, but without divulging that you saw his phone.

However, *l'chatchilah*, when a parent absolutely must get a phone for a child, for whatever reason, there is nothing wrong with informing the child that you intend to check the history of the phone on a constant basis. Then the child is on notice, which makes this a win-win situation.

Keep Him Close to You

Q My son has been doing things that concern me and of which I do not approve. Most recently, a friend from his shiur sent him a link on his phone to watch movies. He is now watching things for many hours and I cannot get him to stop.

He has been begging me all summer to take him to a Yankees game. I have been pushing him off, but eventually I have to give him an answer. What should I tell him?

A Since your son is clearly having *Yiddishkeit* issues, take him, but *davka* so you can show him that he is important to you. In the meantime, keep a close eye on him, and keep the lines of communication open.

Obsessively Learning Is a Warning Sign

Q Our oldest son is thirteen years old. He was always more on the serious side, but he used to play with siblings and friends. In first grade, he decided on his own that he *wanted to go to shul for the entire davening on Shabbos, and he has been doing so ever since. In fourth grade, he started taking Yiddishkeit very seriously. Too seriously. He would tell the boys in his class that they were doing things wrong. He got very into learning and decided that it comes above all else. He stopped playing with his siblings because he has to learn. He stopped eating and sleeping properly because he has to learn.*

Recently, he decided that he knows better than we, his parents, do, so he does not have to listen to us. He recently decided that he doesn't want to go to school because he can learn better at home. He is often found in school learning things other than what is being taught because he feels the need to do more.

We are petrified that he is going to burn out or really damage himself with his behavior. What can we do?

A Your son needs help. Therapy is a must. In the meantime, tell him you are getting him a *chavrusa*, then go out there and hire the most *geshmak'e, frum*-looking *yungerman* to learn with him. Of course, he will be much more than a *chavrusa*. He will be a mentor, buddy, big brother, etc. When this *yungerman* earns your son's confidence, let him take him out to eat and be *mashpia* on your son. As for you, his parents, you must take a hands-off attitude. Don't push him or bother him, but find this person quickly. Children tend not to trust their parents when it comes to such issues. An outsider would be most helpful.

Dealing With a Young Thief

Q *I work in a store in a frum neighborhood and we recently noticed on the cameras an ongoing problem of a thirteen-year-old boy stealing items from the store. It's the same boy who keeps coming back again and again. On the one hand, it must be stopped, and the boy needs to pay for the items he's stolen. However, I don't want to mishandle the situation and cause unnecessary damage to the boy. Can the Rosh Yeshivah give me some guidance as to whether it is best to approach the school or the boy's parents? And the next time the boy comes into the store, what should we say or not say?*

A Sometimes children steal because they are poor, but that does not seem to be the case here. You seem to be dealing with a child with underlying issues. Do not go through the school. You have to worry that they will use this as an excuse to throw the child out. You should speak with the parents. There is always the chance that they will not take it seriously, but you will have done your duty.

Shake Him Up to Stop Stealing

Q *My wife has recently noticed small amounts of money missing around the house, and it seems likely that my thirteen-year-old son is the one taking it. He's a great kid, but he's impulsive, and we've had a few incidents when he was younger. When I brought it up with him casually, he denied it. We don't want to make him feel that he is under suspicion, chas veshalom, especially as I am not one hundred percent sure myself. What should I do?*

A You must sit him down for a major conversation, preferably out of the house and privately. Tell him if this continues, you will not be able to trust him with anything. That may shake him up. If it continues, there are more severe suggestions, but start with this. Hopefully, it will work.

Inappropriate "Show and Tell"

Q My five-year-old son told me that he was in the boys' bathroom in school and he saw two boys in a stall together "showing each other." He said one boy was in his bunk and the other was in an older bunk, though I don't know how old. We briefly discussed that such a thing should never happen, what to say and do if he ever finds himself in a similar situation chas veshalom, and that next time he should tell a morah. I also told him how proud I was of him that he told me, as he was obviously hesitant and ambivalent about sharing this information. I feel a tremendous responsibility to tell the mother of the older boy, as I know he will be in contact with the younger one regularly as they are neighbors. Should I call her? Should I have further conversation about it with my son?

A It sounds to me like you handled this wonderfully. This type of thing is nothing to panic over. When children this young do this, it is just a budding awareness of their bodies. It is only a problem if a kid does this on a regular basis. It is for this reason that the principals and I use the children's bathrooms — to keep an eye out for inappropriate behavior.

I would leave it alone for now. Keep your eyes and ears open and address it only if it happens again.

Secret Internet Access

Q My teenaged son (a yasom) is a confused boy. He is not off the derech, but at risk of becoming so. He dresses fine and doesn't flaunt any misdeeds, but he sleeps all morning, and doesn't daven or learn.

What I am really worried about now is that perhaps there is a device in the picture that I don't know about. He has had a flip phone for a while and we had it filtered by TAG. But for the past few months, he is up past when everyone else is sleeping. I hear him walking around at three or four a.m. He will spend over an hour in the bathroom at that hour. I cannot imagine what he would be doing other than surfing the internet or watching movies (neither of which there is otherwise access to in our home). How can I approach him without accusing him? I tried asking what he does all night and he just said, "Stuff." Can I ask him if he has a device I don't know about?

It is clear that your son has acquired access to the internet; your instincts are correct. You must speak to him in a very soft way, saying that you understand the urge to watch these types of things, but that he will find later as an adult that he has caused himself terrible problems. You can confront him directly, but let him know that you will not punish him if he tells you the truth. You should remain the mother who first and foremost gives him love and kindness and then maybe a little bit of *mussar*.

Meanwhile, you must retain a strong *yungerman* who can become his best friend and mentor. He can officially be a *chavrusa*, but besides learning, he should take him out to eat and for walks and become his confidant. Such a person can accomplish more than a mother can. You should keep your own relationship with your son positive.

Stuck Between a Rock and a Hard Place

Recently, I discussed with Rabbi Bender my eleventh grade son who I thought had a device. When I approached him, he denied it, but I told him that I understand there is a yetzer hara for these kinds of things, and if he ever wants to speak to me about it, I am here. Now, a few weeks later, he approached me and asked if he can get himself a smartphone. He says since he's not in yeshivah, he plans on working and will need one. I told him I would think about it, but if I allow it, we would need proper filters and I would need to have access to his browsing history, to which he agreed. I then asked him if in the past all his internet use was fully kosher, and he finally admitted that he had a device until a few weeks ago, and he used YouTube but all kosher, just sports. (I'm not sure I believe that.) Should I let him have a phone, or am I giving in too easily?

A You are stuck between a rock and a hard place. You must let him get a smartphone because if you don't, he will get one on his own. You then will have zero control over it. This way, you can at least try to make some conditions with him, which hopefully you will be able to put in place. But make sure it is filtered by TAG.

Speaking with Abusive Parents

Q *I have a talmid this year who is very sensitive and will do just about anything for attention. He comes and goes as he pleases, and is extremely sensitive to any instruction or rebuke.*

Last week, he came over to me in the beis medrash and began crying. He said he was wrongfully accused of something, and his mother reprimanded him very harshly. I calmed him down and had a long shmooze with him. Later that day, the menahel told me that the boy approached him as well, and mentioned that he cannot stand listening to his parents fight and argue anymore.

Is there a way the yeshivah could or should approach

the parents and let them know how detrimental their behavior is for their children? Or should we stay out of it? Perhaps the boy is exaggerating, and perhaps it is not our concern?

A You should certainly get involved, and straightaway. You should call the parents in for a meeting and tell them they are killing their son. This is not an exaggeration. However, you must first make sure that they will not take this out on their son. If they will, you must find another way. But there is no reason they should not be told. They must realize the damage they are doing. If they are wise and reasonable, they will thank you in the long term.

A Matter
of Faith

Strengthening Emunah
in Times of Trouble

Q What message should we be giving our children regarding the current matzav in general?

A The question is how much *emunah* to teach. In the girls' schools more is taught, but in general, we hesitate to address the topic since too many questions are raised. However, this is an opportunity to talk about *emunah*. We have no idea why this is happening, but there is a *HaKadosh Baruch Hu*. There is no *gilui panim*, only *hester panim*. We have to make sure to connect in our *tefillos*. There is a *gezeirah* going on and we don't understand it, but we must daven to break the *gezeirah*. We can't even try to give reasons.

When we were hit with Hurricane Sandy, there was conjecture (after we made a major burial of ruined *sefarim*) that maybe we were hit by the waters of the ocean because we don't care enough about our *sefarim*. I was unhappy with that. Last I heard, we don't have people with *ruach hakodesh* all over the world! How can anyone say that they know the reason! We don't know the reasons of the *Eibishter*. What I have noticed is that people have *dei'os* and *shittos*. And they then use their pet theory as the excuse for all evils that may *chas veshalom* invade our homes.

We can give *chizuk*. Strengthening behavior in shul, not talking in shul, not running around — all that is in order. We can be *mechazek emunah* and *bitachon*. Some children have the misguided impression that Hashem is mean because of *s'char v'onesh*. He is not mean, but rather He is doing what is best for the world and we cannot fathom the reason. The people who died are sitting in a wonderful place in Gan Eden, though we are suffering from the loss of these people. Depending on the age of the person we are addressing, we can speak about these things.

We Don't Have to Know the Answers

Q *I understand that everything is for the good, but that doesn't make me feel calm. Because if everything is good, what's next? Painful things can continue to happen to me because Hashem decided they're good. How am I supposed to trust?*

A This is a question that has bothered our greatest leaders for thousands of years. In the first fifteen *perakim* of *Tehillim*, no less a person than David HaMelech asks this question again and again. Why do evil people have so much good and great people have so much difficulty? Without *emunah* and *bitachon*, one cannot answer this question. It is impossible to explain why these things happen, but we know Hashem has a plan for everything.

I have no idea why my father passed away when I was fifteen years old, but I do know that my brave mother picked up the pieces, and together, we had a beautiful home. I also know that one day my questions will be answered. Does that mean that one should not feel bad when painful things happen? We are all normal human beings! But we march on, because that is what we have to do.

As far as stopping to worry, I once read a poem in which the poet wrote, "Don't walk, you might fall. Don't run, you might trip. Don't live, you might die…" If we worry constantly, there is no life. We have to believe that there is a very bright future ahead of us. That is what kept me going all the years, and it is what will keep you going too.

Asking Hashem for Reasons and Enlightenment

Q *I once heard that we aren't allowed to ask Hashem why certain things happen to us, but sometimes I just really want to ask why. Can we ask Hashem why things happen?*

A It is absolutely untrue that you cannot ask Hashem. But rephrase it. After you ask Hashem why things happen, ask Him to help you find the reasons and to enlighten you. There is nothing wrong with that. Hashem knows we are not robots. We are people with emotions and feelings. You know what? Hashem created those emotions and feelings in us. It is perfectly fine to seek answers.

Does Hashem Love Us?

Q *Children ask, "If HaKadosh Baruch Hu loves us so much, why is He doing this to us?" How do we respond?*

A We cannot answer that question other than to explain, to the best of our abilities, that He absolutely loves us one hundred percent. Reference the words in *Krias Shema*. At the same time, Hashem may want us to be *mechazek* in certain areas. "But He absolutely loves us. Hashem is not mean! He knows what we need. One day we will merit to know the answers."

Keep Your Connection to Hashem

Q *I davened so hard that my mother should get better. I cried and begged. But Hashem said no, and she passed away. I took the lesson from this to daven for something once and stop there. If Hashem says no, who am I to daven and beg again?*

A Moshe Rabbeinu desperately wanted to go into Eretz Yisrael. He too cried and begged, so to speak. He tried five hundred and fifteen separate times! Hashem had to tell him to stop asking. And his reason was only that he wanted so badly to do those mitzvos that one can only fulfill in Eretz Yisrael! You may daven for the things you want again and again. Don't forget that Hashem is the *Avi yesomos*. You might not feel it, but He is watching out for you more than you can possibly know!

Living With Emunah After Tragedy

Q *I hear a lot of, "We don't understand Hashem's ways," or "We need to accept this…" How do I live with emunah after my father passed away? What if I really don't get why he had to die? I really don't understand, and I have a hard time accepting it.*

A This is not something to try to understand at this time. David HaMelech asks this question again and again in *Tehillim*. In fact, many of the early *perakim* refer to this issue. And David HaMelech basically says, we must wait for answers. That is what *emunah* is all about.

I lived it. All *yesomim* and *yesomos* live it. We need time. Time does heal, and as you get older, you may begin to understand it just a little bit.

Reclaiming My Connection to Hashem

Q It's very hard for me to develop a connection with Hashem these days. Now that the Yamim Tovim are approaching, it bothers me even more. Last Rosh Hashanah I davened really hard for a good year. My mother was very sick and I was so hoping she'd get better. But she didn't, and was nifteres. This year has been very difficult for me, and I'm in a lot of pain. How can I reclaim my connection with Hashem?

A You are not the only one who has a hard time connecting to Hashem. Many of us don't feel Hashem because He is not here in the physical sense. When situations are painful for us, we feel lost. But you must try to remember that there is a Master Plan.

I have the *zechus* in my office to work with a very special woman. She has extraordinary *emunah* and *bitachon* in Hashem and I see it tangibly daily with her. She lost her young husband at the age of 43 to a heart attack. She lost a young daughter at the age of 22, suddenly. She lost a 46-year-old son to cancer. He left many *yesomim* and *yesomos*. Yet, she has such faith in Hashem! She has such unbelievable *simchas hachaim*. She shines daily and exudes happiness. How can she do this? I think she realizes we are just passing through this world. When Mashiach comes, there will be a one-thousand-piece philharmonic orchestra greeting her. She will be the poster girl for *bitachon*. Then the world will see what the *Ribbono Shel Olam* appreciates!

I would like to tell you something interesting. A close friend of mine, a leader in *Klal Yisrael,* told me recently, "Hashem made you a young *yasom* so you could feel the pain of young widows and *yesomim* today." It was very difficult for me to hear this. But it could very well be true. Personally, I don't think this is correct. I always felt the reason why I give a bit of time to widows and orphans is because I used to hear a lot on this topic from my mother and father when I was very young. But it doesn't matter. I can certainly identify with the pains of a *yasom* because I lived it.

Try the following. Don't daven to Hashem. Have a conversation with Him. Ask Him questions in a *b'kavodig* fashion. The answers will come, but not overnight.

Turn to Hashem When in Pain

Q *The pasuk says that one must be very careful not to cause pain to an almanah or yasom because if they cry out, Hashem will listen to them. I was wondering, if someone causes me pain, is it okay to cry out even though I don't want them to receive any punishment because of me? After all, I'm still in pain.*

A You should never feel guilty for crying out to Hashem, whether in the midst of a *tzarah* or afterward. Hashem is there to listen at all times. You can specifically ask that He not punish the other person, but always turn to Hashem.

How Can I Know What Hashem Wants From Me?

Q *How am I supposed to know what Hashem wants from me? I'm already missing a major guide in navigating my*

*life since my mother died. So how am I supposed to fig-
ure it out?*

A There are a number of *sefarim* and books published in the
past few years about how to deal with grief. Many give
excellent *hadrachah*. Choose the book that speaks to you
best, read it again and again, and you will start to figure out some
answers. This is much too difficult to respond to in a question-
and-answer format, as there is no one simple answer to this
question.

Asking for a Sign From Shamayim

Q *Are you allowed to ask for a sign that your deceased parent is still there? I need my parent's reassurance that
they're still around for me.*

A Your parents are always watching out for you, even after
they are *niftar*. Unfortunately, you cannot see it or understand it. But we must trust Chazal. Somehow, the *yesomos* and *yesomim* I know have tremendous *siyata diShmaya* and
hatzlachah. That is because of two reasons: (1) Hashem is the *Avi
yesomim*. (2) Your parent is watching over you and going to bat for
you in *Shamayim*.

However, asking for a sign is a very dangerous thing. We hear
so many great stories about people asking for signs and how they
were answered. Ninety-five percent of these stories are not true.
Are there some great people or even not such great people who see
a sign when they ask for it? Yes, but these are few and far between.
If we start down this path, there will be devastation when people
don't receive these signs. Be careful. Just know *Hakadosh Baruch
Hu* is looking out for you.

Hashem, Please Lighten My Burden

Q *I was always taught that Hashem only does what's best. Well, intellectually I understand that it's good for me that my father passed away and left my mother to care for me and my many siblings. But where does davening come in? If it's all good, the hardships that come along with losing a father — and there are many — then what am I davening for?*

A You are talking to someone who has been there and done that. Some questions we will not have full answers to in this world. My Rosh Yeshivah, Rav Shmuel Berenbaum, lost two sons during his lifetime. Though he grieved long and hard for his two buried children, Rav Berenbaum chose to move on with his life. It takes great people to understand what Hashem wants from us. Most of us don't. With time, *iy"H*, things will become easier. In the meantime, just ask Hashem to lighten your burden so you can learn how to smile once again. Ask Him for nothing else. *Iy"H*, one day you will connect better.

Struggling With Suffering

Q *While we were sitting shivah for my mother, a rebbetzin trying to give us chizuk told us how special we are, that only tzidkaniyos go through struggles. She said that Hashem wants a closer connection with us and wants our tefillos even more. She went on to say that the Imahos were akaros because Hashem wanted their tefillos. I'm not sure I'm allowed to ask this question, but is it fair?*

A I would not have given you that answer. Of course, everything the rebbetzin said is true, but that is not what should be said when people are sitting *shivah*.

Chazal tell us that originally, the brain was made in such a way that we would remember everything. Then, when Hashem saw that people would grieve their entire lives, He decided to create *shikchah*, forgetfulness. That is really a blessing in disguise. This is a question you should not seek an answer to now. The loss is too fresh. One day, when you are older, you will delve into it. But realize it will not be easy to find and accept the answers.

In the meantime, remember these three things: (1) Hashem is watching over you. (2) Your mother is watching over you. (3) Don't feel bad for your mother; she is in a better place.

One day, *b'ezras Hashem*, you will be reunited.

Mitzvos for All Situations

Q As an older single girl, I must ask, why are the mitzvos geared primarily to people with families?

A Hashem created the world for its creations to procreate and multiply. Sometimes, He decides that certain people should not. Just a few examples: the Chazon Ish, Rav Shlomo Heiman, the Lubavitcher Rebbe, etc. Yet, these people were shining lights to the entire world. We do not decide who, what, when, or where. But we march on, secure in our *bitachon* in the *Ribbono Shel Olam*.

Many mitzvos are there for certain circumstances: e.g., *mitzvos hateluyos baAretz*, which apply only to those people living in Eretz Yisrael; and mitzvos that apply only in the time of the Beis HaMikdash. The Torah is our guidebook for life. Whatever applies, we do. Period.

Vital Message in the Haggadah

Q *Which piece of the Haggadah really speaks to you and why?*

A The most significant piece to me is *V'hi She'amdah,* which tells us that no matter what befalls us, we will always end by standing upright, strong, and healthy. My mother *a"h* used to come to us for Pesach and tell my children stories of Europe during World War II and pre-WW II. Nowadays, I continue that by telling my children and grandchildren stories about our parents and grandparents who experienced very difficult times in their lives. Yet we are all here today, celebrating Pesach.

When speaking with our children, we cannot deny the difficulties our nation has faced, but *V'hi She'amdah* does somewhat help in explaining it. It is certainly a very strong message for all young people. As difficult as life seems sometimes, with Hashem's help, you will make it — big time!

Understanding Why We Daven

Q *What is our job when we daven? Are we just asking Hashem to do things for us, or thanking Him or praising Him?*

A The answer is all three. We thank Hashem, and we have the privilege to ask Him for anything we need, even if it is a small thing. I don't think that, if you are a Yankee fan, you should ask Hashem that the Yankees should win the World Series next year, or if you are a football Giants fan, that you should ask Him that they should finally win a few games. But let's say someone in your house has a cold. You can certainly have him in mind while reciting the *berachah* of *Refa'einu.*

The question really is, what is davening all about? Davening is hard because we don't see Hashem, and He's therefore abstract to us. When we daven, we can focus on Him. When we say the words, "*Baruch Atah Hashem*," we think, "*Gebentched are You, Hashem.*"

In the first set of *berachos* of *Shemoneh Esrei*, there's the *berachah* of *Magen Avos* where we say that we have the *zechus* of Avraham, Yitzchak, and Yaakov. The second *berachah* is about *techiyas hameisim*. It is called *gevurah* because it speaks about the *gevurah* of *Hakadosh Baruch Hu*. We then say "*Atah kadosh.*" We are saying, "You, Hashem, are awesome and holy, and we love You."

At the end of *Shemoneh Esrei* we begin a *berachah* saying, *Modim anachnu lach*, and conclude the *berachah* by saying, *Hatov Shimcha u'lecha naeh l'hodos*, Hashem, we love You and thank You because You take care of us. Then in *Sim shalom*, we ask Hashem to inject peace into the world.

There are a total of nineteen *berachos*. (*V'LaMalshinim* is a later addition.) The middle thirteen *berachos*, beginning with "*Atah chonein*," are where we ask Hashem to help us. We ask Him to give us a good intellect to learn his Torah. "*Hashiveinu Avinu l'sorasecha*," we ask Hashem to bring us back to His Torah. In "*Selach lanu*" we ask Hashem to forgive us for our sins. "*Refa'einu Hashem v'neirafeh*," Hashem, please send a *refuah sheleimah* to all those who are not well. "*Bareich aleinu*," bless our work so that we should have *parnassah*. "*T'ka b'shofar gadol*," please blow the shofar of Eliyahu HaNavi and bring Mashiach.

And of course, we have *Shema Koleinu*. You can ask for anything here. This is the best place, before you say, "*Ki Atah shomei'a….*" You can say, "My mother is not feeling well. Please grant her a *refuah sheleimah.*" You can make specific requests during other *berachos* as well — for health in *Refa'einu*, for *parnassah* in *Bareich Aleinu*, but to simplify matters, you can request everything in the *berachah* of *Shema Koleinu*. In that *berachah*, we ask Hashem to hear our voices and have pity on us. We need health. We need *parnassah*. We want to learn Torah with *geshmak*. Perhaps someone is depressed — please, Hashem, take me out of my depression.

Speak in any language, in your own words, during the thirteen *berachos*. Hashem understands them all. You cannot add your own words during the first three or the last three *berachos*. But during the middle thirteen *berachos*, you can add anything you want, especially in *Shema Koleinu*, though there are some opinions in Chazal not to overdo this. You can also make requests at the end of *Elokai Netzor*. Use the opportunity to connect. When you talk to *HaKadosh Baruch Hu* and make requests, you are connecting, and then you can also thank Him.

Middos, the Measure of Man

Stressing Basic Derech Eretz

Q I am a teacher in a boys' school, and several times I have noted the boys' lack of basic derech eretz. Recently, I was leaving the building and I was literally injured by a boy smashing into me as he ran into the building. The reb-beim do not seem to be taking a strong stand in making them be more respectful. What can be done about this?

A Unfortunately, this is an everyday occurrence with boys. You must speak to the *hanhalah*. The boys' behavior ulti-mately reflects on the administration; maybe they will be moved to do something about it. I don't think the boys mean any-thing bad, they are just not thinking. There must be constant *shmuessen* in yeshivos to talk about it. This cannot be combatted with just a *shmuess* once in a while. There must be ongoing incul-cation of *middos tovos*!

Expecting Good Sportsmanship

Q My family is big into games. We enjoy playing board games as a family, and my kids often invite friends over to play games as well. While most of us are mainly involved for the fun and camaraderie, I have one son who is extremely competitive. He takes playing games to an extreme, competing fiercely and focusing intently on the goal: winning. When he does win, which is often, he expresses his triumph vocally, and I'm concerned that he doesn't realize his friends or siblings might be upset. How can I help him become a more empathetic winner and react differently even in the excitement of achieving the highest score?

A This is essentially a *middos* question, and it is very difficult to change a *middah*. Rav Yisrael Salanter says it is easier to learn the entire *Shas* than to change one *middah*.

First of all, playing to win is perfectly fine. I never understood when *mechanchim* would say, "It's not important who wins; it's important to enjoy yourself." Let me tell you a secret. If you don't play to win, the game is a disaster. Kids love to play ball with competition, and they are playing to win. And that is perfectly fine.

Then there is another piece called sportsmanship. It is our job to teach our children to never, ever, ever make fun of other children, gloat, show off, or rejoice at another's defeat. Play to win and go for it, but only with *middos tovos*.

Lying Is Common in Very Young Children

Q My five-year-old son is a very good and geshmak'e kid both at home and at school, baruch Hashem. Lately, though, he's been not emesdig left and right, making up detailed stories that are far from the truth on a regular basis, sometimes even when we ask regular everyday questions. For example, after he got hurt the other day, I asked him if he asked the rebbi to call me and he said that he asked, but the rebbi said that they couldn't call because they were learning important things right now. But the rebbi said he never asked to call me.

A At first, you sit with him and explain why *sheker* is a bad thing. This is not serious; it is very common with pre-school-aged children. If his lying becomes more serious, there are very strong *eitzos*. But based on this story, I would not get excited at all.

Learning About Emes the Right Way

Q Our three-year-old daughter received a chart from her morah. She filled it out on her own, without our knowledge, and redeemed it for a prize from her morah. When she came home, she told me exactly what she did. My husband feels that since it has happened a few times before that she wasn't honest, we should make her own up and return the prize to teach her a lesson about honesty. I feel that since we are working hard with her on behavior in general, this can be overlooked, especially as she doesn't seem to realize what was wrong with it.

A Don't make her return the prize; just explain what she did wrong. She clearly doesn't understand that she did something wrong, as witnessed by the fact that she told you all about it! She is quite young. She will mature, hopefully, as most children do. Buy her a couple of books on *emes* and read them to her. She will soon get the idea.

Truthfulness Training

Q Recently, my daughter who is nearly six has been having an issue with the truth, making things up in a very deceptive way. For example, our younger son had a mark on his hand that he clearly didn't make himself. It was clear that it was from his sister. She denied it. Usually, her denials are in situations when she is concerned for herself.

A If it happens only once in a while, spend some time discussing and reading about *emes* with her. If it becomes chronic even when she is over seven years old, Rav Hutner says for three days, don't believe anything she says. If she says, "I'm hungry," respond, "I don't believe you." "My classmate hurt me." "I don't believe you." But you must be consistent. After three days, she will get the message.

Cruelty Must Be Addressed

Q My husband died several years ago, and my daughter is now in ninth grade. There is a girl in her class who seems to like to remind my daughter that she has no father. For example, when my daughter complained about her math homework, this girl said, very loudly and purposefully, "Oh. Well, my father helps me."

Yesterday, on the bus, this girl sat next to my daughter and began to sing a song about orphans and widows.

When my daughter gave her a look, she said, "Oh, I know why you're glaring at me. You're so over-sensitive. I can sing a song if I want to."

My daughter is not willing to confront the girl and begged me not to involve the school or her parents, as she will make a huge scene if it gets brought up. But what else can I do?

This is a blatant and repugnant thing for someone to do, and the school MUST be involved. If this happened in my school, I would give a fiery lecture to the entire high school about what it means to be cruel to anyone, especially a *yesomah*. I would explain the sensitivity of a *yesomah* and what the Torah says about hurting such a person. Then I would verbally slaughter this individual for making fun of an orphan, without picking out the perpetrator. If your daughter will not speak up herself, this girl had better be straightened out some other way. If she retains this type of cruelty and rotten *middos*, then when she gets married, she will be divorced within a month.

It's Normal to Feel Jealous — But Look at the Whole Picture

How can I keep from being jealous of those who have what I lack? Am I a bad person for feeling jealous?

The *baalei mussar* say that the most difficult *middah* to eradicate is jealousy. It is a perfectly normal reaction of sane people. The issue is that we may be jealous when we see what the other has, but we don't really know what is going on in their lives. If we did, we would not be jealous.

One summer, on visiting day, the head counselor of Camp Bonim told me about a conversation he'd overheard. On visiting day, a long white limousine had approached the camp gate. The impressive car had continued up the hill, past the sign that read, "No cars allowed beyond this point." It had even driven onto the grass, headed for the bunk area. A group of parents standing near the dining room looked on. "If you have money, then I guess you don't have to follow the rules," one man commented bitterly.

That was the exchange the head counselor shared with me. We both knew the details and background of that white limousine and its journey into the middle of the camp. There was a young father in Lakewood who was ravaged by illness, his life quickly ebbing away. His children were in camp with us, and some generous friends decided that this man must see his children on visiting day. He was in too much pain to travel in an ambulance, so they rented an extra-stretch limousine and removed the seats. They installed a bed and sent a nurse along to attend to him. The boys were excited to see their father, and also for him to see them and how they were living for the summer. The children wanted him to see their bunk, so the car was allowed to pull up to the bunkhouse where the door was opened so the father could look inside.

"You have an amazing bunk. I love seeing it," he told his beloved children.

He passed away right after camp.

It was a dramatic, powerful, deeply moving scene, an enduring image of pain fused with the kindness of *Klal Yisrael* and the love of a father for his children. But those parents, drinking coffee and watching, only saw that people in expensive cars can break the rules. Because they didn't have eyes to see what they themselves had, only what they did not have, that car was a challenge to them. Had they known the whole story, they would not have been jealous of that long white car and its passenger.

What Constitutes Maaser Zman?

Q *I heard that Rav Moshe Feinstein said that every person must give maaser not only of money but also of time. He recommended using ten percent of one's time for chessed. I later heard from Rav Bluth that Rav Moshe said he himself gave about fifty percent of his time for chessed. Rav Bluth asked if that was because of all the shailos he answered for people, and Rav Moshe replied that, no, that was part of learning.*

Rav Moshe was learning, davening, and answering shailos for twelve hours a day. Did he do chessed the other twelve? I am wondering how this is possible and exactly what is included as chessed.

A I think you cannot bring any proof from Rav Feinstein. He was a *malach*! I discussed it with Rabbi Yisroel Kleinman, who tells me Rav Moshe's *lashon* was, "*fuftzik pertzent ich geb avek tzu ton far yenem,*" loosely translated, "fifty percent of my time I give away to do for others." Rav Moshe didn't say that he gave fifty percent of his time for *chessed. Chessed* in the form of "*tzu ton far yenem*" isn't only delivering Tomchei Shabbos or being in Hatzolah. To discuss a concern with someone or *chap* a two-minute shmooze to make someone's day, to acknowledge him and make him feel relevant, is doing for *yenem.*

Rav Bluth says any Rosh Yeshivah or Rav or anyone involved in *klal* work is giving at least fifty percent *far yenem.* Rav Chaim Kanievsky makes himself *hefker* aside from the morning hours that he locks himself in his room. Rav Shneur did it. R' Dovid did it. *Yb"l* Rav Reuven and others still do this. Rebbeim and *klal* people are all about *yenem.*

Anyone who keeps the people around him on his radar and looks to make eye contact and give a smile is giving time for *chessed.* Broaden the scope to call a neighbor or elderly shut-in and your "*ton far yenem*" quotient goes up even more.

Middos, the Measure of Man 267

If a person is committed to helping people, he will find the time. I know someone who gives two *shiurim* and three *shmuessen* weekly, a very busy rebbi with many obligations. He wanted to do *daf yomi*. He did not have the time. But he found a way to make the time. He never sits around after a *chuppah*. Instead, he has hiding places in every hall to sit and learn. I think for *chessed* also, find a way. The world says, if you want something done, give it to a busy person.

Taking a Respectful Stand

Q My children are trained to stand up every single time either of their parents walks into the room. On the one hand, we don't want to stop them from this big mitzvah and hergesh they have. On the other hand, I hate the tirchah involved for their sake and want them to be normal and do only what is halachically required. I am also afraid they will come to resent being interrupted so many times during their games or whatnot.

A This is a very beautiful thing, but you are right, they should not stand up every single time. They can stand up once a day, unless there are other people present. Then they should stand. It is the appropriate thing to do. Don't worry about the *tirchah*. It will not be to their detriment.

Is it Still a Chessed If Payment Is Accepted?

Q A mother in our neighborhood recently had surgery and my twelve-year-old daughter went to help out for a few hours. On her way out, they gave her twenty dollars. My *daughter told us she would rather not accept the money and just do it as a chessed. Should we allow her to return the money so that she feels she did a chessed, or should we encourage her to keep it so they feel comfortable asking her for help again if they need it?*

A If she doesn't want to accept the money, let her return it. *Chessed* is *chessed*. However, as her parents, show recognition of what she is doing by buying her a small gift. Have no worry about them calling her back. If she did a good job, the family will definitely call her back should the need arise.

Responding to the Silent Treatment

Q *I am divorced with five children and we live in Israel. My fifteen-year-old son dorms during the week and comes home for Shabbos. A few weeks ago, two friends of mine, both single women, offered to take our family to a hotel in Tzefas for Shabbos. I assumed that my son would not join us, as he usually avoids situations where many girls and women will be present, but he surprised me by saying he would join. I assumed there was something brewing, and indeed, several of his friends from yeshivah were in Tzefas for Shabbos and he spent much of Shabbos with them. In general, he behaved very maturely at the seudos, making Kiddush, saying divrei Torah, and singing zemiros.*

However, on Motza'ei Shabbos, he was with his friends and didn't come back for a long time. We did all the packing and shlepping without him. He called and asked me to pack his things and bring them to him as he was a twenty-minute walk away. I refused, saying we could not make our hosts wait or impose on them and take them out of their way. He said, "If you don't bring my things, I will not walk into your house again for a year." In the end, he made other arrangements to pick up his things and took the bus back to yeshivah as we had planned.

On Sunday, I called him to say, "Even though I had to be tough, I still love you." He said, "I can't talk to you. By me you did a pesha," and hung up. I tried a few more times over the next several weeks; he will not come to the phone. I called his Rosh Yeshivah, who agreed with me that his response was not okay. He tried to talk to my son about it, but my son said he needs some time. He is very close with one of the rebbeim in the area and I know I can talk to him, but I think my son will resent me even more for making him look bad in the eyes of his rebbi.

I'm concerned about his akshanus, his lack of respect, sense of entitlement, and tendency to shut down completely when criticized. This is all the more challenging as his father is not a healthy person.

How do I proceed? Should I wait for him to make the first move? Should I try to send him a package with the things I usually give him when he comes home?

A You are in a tricky position, but I will try to address this as best I can. There is nothing wrong with your son spending most of his time with his friends. This is very normal for a boy his age, especially as, by your own admission, he was at the *seudos* and behaved very nicely at them. Based on his behavior over Shabbos, I would perhaps have recommended that you try to accommodate him on Motza'ei Shabbos. However, his response is unacceptable.

That being said, you cannot force the issue. You need to give him time and space. By all means, send him a package. Beyond that, give it at least another month. Then we can revisit the issue. *Middos* are not easily changed and you may need to be patient with him, especially given the circumstances.

Should Middos Affect Hiring?

Q A young man applied for a job as a counselor in our day camp. His rebbi said the nicest things about him. But I happen to know this boy a bit. His family ate at our house once and he was very mean and tough with his mother and sister. Should I hire him?

A On the one hand, you need to tell him directly that you did not approve of his *kibbud eim* and the way he treated his sister when he was at your house. Ask how he thinks this will affect his job as a counselor. Listen to his answer and then decide. But warn him that at the first infraction, he may lose his job.

On the other hand, there are certain kids that may misbehave at home, for a variety of reasons, such as a total lack of discipline or otherwise, but are perfectly well-behaved in school or in camp. *Lav davka* that I would not accept him as a counselor.

When an Ex Is Involved

Sending Our Nephew to Yeshivah

Q My brother is divorced and remarried. His son is fourteen and in ninth grade. During the week, he lives with his mother who is not shomer Shabbos. On Shabbos, he is with his father.

For the past year, my nephew has been coming to our house for Shabbos, going to the netz minyan and shiurim with my husband. He really loves learning and the feeling of Shabbos that he experiences in our home. He currently goes to yeshivah, but his mother wants to take him out and put him in public school because she feels the yeshivah does not challenge him enough.

His father says that if his ex-wife won't pay for yeshivah, neither will he. I spoke to my husband and said that if we can afford it, I would be happy to cut something out of our lives and pay some amount every month to enable our nephew to continue in yeshivah.

My husband spoke to our Rav who said that if the parents don't care enough to invest in their son's neshamah (when the issue is not financial) then it's not our place to intervene. I understand that it's not my place, but I can't just sit back and let my nephew waste his life away in public school. I feel like if he goes to public school, he will be lost forever.

A I don't understand your Rabbi at all. If this child were not your nephew, but lived down the block, you would have to intervene on his behalf. The *achrayus* of every *neshamah* in *Klal Yisrael* is "ours" collectively. The Gemara in *Bava Basra* tells us that Yehoshua ben Gamla is credited with saving *Klal Yisrael* because he made yeshivos for those children who had no one to teach them Torah, such as *yesomim*. Furthermore, the Gemara tells us there that were it not for Yehoshua ben Gamla, *nishtakach Torah m'Yisrael*, Torah would have been forgotten from *Klal Yisrael*.

My *rebbi*, Rav Yisroel Belsky *zt"l*, once asked: Why would Torah have been forgotten from *Klal Yisrael*? Only those children who would not have learned would have forgotten the Torah. He answered that if those kids who couldn't learn through no fault of their own would have forgotten Torah, then Torah would have been lost from the entire nation!

Not only should you help, it is a *chiyuv* for everyone in Klal Yisrael to help. You are doing the right thing.

One day, you will have tremendous *nachas b'ezras Hashem*.

Abide by the Schedule

Q *I was recently divorced and have a question about Shabbos with my sons. Most of the time, when I "have them" for Shabbos, they eat with me and sleep in their mother's house. (I live close to my ex-wife.) This week, however, I told my sons that I would like to take them to Lakewood to their sister's house. My sons told me that they want to stay home because they don't want to miss the Shabbos learning with their rebbi. I usually do what they want to do, but I feel it needs to be explained to them that if their father requests something, they should be mekabel. They need to understand that I am human as well.*

A Let them be. On the weeks that you have them, you should adhere to their schedule. Go to Lakewood another week. Kids in this situation are always torn apart with guilt. Our job is to make them feel happy and comfortable. Your sons are children and are the biggest *korbanos* in the matter. It is not their job to ease the situation for you. They do not need the extra pressure.

Don't Move Closer to Ex-Husband for Child's Sake

Q *I am divorced and have an eight-year-old son. My ex-husband lives in Israel. My son spends vacations there. Baruch Hashem, he is in therapy and has an excellent mentor.*

The last time my son returned from Israel, he was very angry with me. He is upset that he lives so far away from all his relatives in Israel and blames me. Do I have to consider moving overseas? My entire family and support system are here in New York.

A You should not move overseas. You must stay where your support network is. You must take care of yourself first so that you can take care of your kids. This is analogous to putting your own oxygen mask on first on the plane. As a

Yiddishe mamme, you must find the right words to comfort your son and explain this to him, but you cannot turn your life over for this.

This letter cannot deal with the myriad of issues that come up in divorce. But one of the most common issues is that when a child comes back from his father, he kvetches, complains, and is angry. The reasons are obvious. Most of all, remember, the father gives him a good time, takes him for pizza, and generally spoils the child somewhat. You have the daily regular chores and drudgery, such as insisting they take a bath or shower, have a normal bedtime, do their homework, wake up on time, and many other things. Don't worry. Most kids figure out in the long run that their mother is providing safety and stability.

I don't think his issue is that he wants to live near his family. His issue is, in his own mind, that when he goes to his father, he is ALWAYS having fun. So he identifies his father and Eretz Yisrael with having more fun than when he is with you.

Ex Allows Internet Access

Q My ex and I agreed that my daughter needed a phone so that we could each communicate with her when she was with the other parent. I wanted an old-fashioned phone but he wanted the most technologically advanced. Somehow, we reached a compromise with our mediator on a smartphone that he would not connect to the internet. Of course, this condition was not kept, so I took away the phone.

My ex is not frum anymore. He was unfortunately abused as a child and now suffers from narcissistic personality disorder. My daughter is terrified of him. She was not supposed to tell me that he allowed her access to the internet and television. What can I do?

A Unfortunately, this problem of one parent leaving the *frumkeit* fold is very common. We have to try very hard to choose the least of all the evils when we are *mechanech* our children in such a situation.

You should not take away her phone. Filter it, monitor what she is watching. But you cannot suddenly come down on her so hard. You don't want to push her into her father's arms. I understand what you are going through, but you must do things slowly and with *seichel*.

Learning With Father Taken to the Extreme

Q My ex insists that his boys call him every single night to learn on the phone. While I am happy he learns with my sons and I certainly value learning in general, he is using this as a controlling mechanism. When I suggest it might be inconvenient one night, they tell me, as if parroting, "It is a mitzvah to learn Torah with your father every day..."

While I was on vacation with them, they started calling their father twice a day, once to tell him what they did that day, and then another time separately to learn.

Things have come to a head now that they are in sleepaway camp. I had hoped that while in camp they would get a break from this, but I have found out that even in camp, they are calling their father every night to learn. They are borrowing their counselors' phones because obviously, campers don't have access to phones on such a regular basis. I am really upset. Is this okay? Should I just look the other way?

First, count your blessings that your husband is diligent about learning with his sons. But everything should be with *seichel* and in moderation. This system becomes a pressure cooker on the boys, and on you. While learning is excellent, when it becomes a chore, it's not healthy. The boys should learn with their father three times a week; that would be sufficient. If one of them has a test the next day, you can make an exception. The learning in camp is detrimental. It takes the children away from their bunkmates' activities. If their father wants to shmooze with them once a week, that is fine. It is critically important for a child from a divorced home to grow up normally. It is not normal to call one's father every day from camp to learn.

Chavrusa/Mentor May Be the Solution

Raising my son with the insidious opposition of my ex-husband has become nearly impossible. My sixth-grade son has not done anything all year in school. But any time I attempt to encourage him, I get shot down by my ex. He also stays out very late at night without telling me where he is. Again, when I try to explain that this is not acceptable, my ex validates my son. Any time I try to assert my authority, my ex undermines me. I feel that I am losing my son. What can I do?

It is very difficult to answer this from far away. You must retain a *geshmak'e*, mature *yungerman* who will officially be his *chavrusa*, but in reality will be his mentor and best friend. You cannot succeed on your own with your son because of your ex and because of adolescence. Adolescence is hard enough on its own. Combined with the other issues, we have a real problem. Go out and find someone quickly. It may be the only way to save your son before things escalate.

Counteracting Dangers to My Child's Chinuch

Q I am divorced, and my ex-husband is no longer frum. He has a girlfriend who is not frum who has a daughter my daughter's age who is in public school. I read my daughter's texts sometimes, and I see that she is using curse words and fantasizing about wearing pants and meeting boys.

Baruch Hashem, there is a wonderful teacher in her school who has been talking to my daughter for the past several months. I continue to go for therapy and to shower my daughter with love and attention. And, of course, I am davening. Is there anything else I should be doing?

A You are doing everything one hundred percent perfectly. All you can do is continue to shower her with love and attention and hope your ex comes to his senses. And of course, continue to daven hard. Hashem wants to hear from you.

Follow up:

Q Unfortunately, the situation has deteriorated. My daughter is thirteen now and she is dressing differently, and when she is with my ex she is watching movies that I would never allow.

A You must get her a young woman to become her best friend/mentor/guidance counselor. Because of your situation with your ex, you may not speak badly about him. It may cost financially, but there is no other solution. Keep on davening and hopefully, your daughter will come around. I have seen *yeshuos* in these types of situations.

Help in Straddling Two Worlds

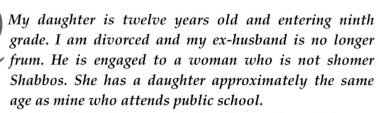

My daughter is twelve years old and entering ninth grade. I am divorced and my ex-husband is no longer frum. He is engaged to a woman who is not shomer Shabbos. She has a daughter approximately the same age as mine who attends public school.

Baruch Hashem, my daughter had an incredibly supportive, non-judgmental teacher last year who has been her mentor, and she has grown tremendously. She has given up some of her "goyish" things and davens on her own sometimes.

From my end, I am spending a lot of quality time with her, with only love, no criticism when she does things like wear pants in the house, even to the Shabbos table. I overlook everything you told me to, while trying to be a role model for her.

It's very obvious that she is straddling two worlds. While with me, she has a genuine love of Yiddishkeit and will spend hours reading Aish.com and such things. We had beautiful Sedarim on Pesach (even though it was just the two of us because of Corona).

I believe she has a true yearning to be ehrlich, but all our hard work gets undone when she goes to her father. She feels beneath them and frumpy (though she is beautiful and put together). Unfortunately, she has been seen wearing short skirts and leggings while with them. Through nissim, she got into a reputable Bais Yaakov, and I'm afraid they will kick her out before she even starts based on her mistakes.

Do you think it would be a good idea for our mediator to tell my ex that this is damaging to our daughter? (It cannot be coming from me as this will goad him further.) I know I cannot control this and must daven and *do my best. Ultimately, the results are up to Hashem, no matter what I do. But would this be considered good hishtadlus?*

There is nothing wrong with having the mediator speak to your husband. Not in a threatening way, but just for him to understand what must be going on in your daughter's mind. Ask him to help keep her sane and healthy. Hopefully, once she starts high school, your daughter will want to be like her classmates. It is essential that you keep your positive relationship with her! And once she starts school, you must find another young teacher to be a role model and mentor for her.

Outside Help Needed to Fight Abuse

I am a divorced mother of four children. I have reason to worry about the time that they spend with their father, due to verbal and emotional abuse, as well as emotional and mental swings that he has. At the same time, I know that having a relationship with one's father is extremely important, and I don't want to take that away from my children if that is what's best for them. They have been coming home telling me of various incidents that concern me. I want to protect them, but don't want to hurt them in the process.

Your children must have an outside person to speak to, a teacher, Rabbi, or therapist, etc., who can determine if they should continue seeing their father. You may then have a legal battle to fight, but that is the first step.

Yesomim

אֲבִי יְתוֹמִים וְדַיַּן אַלְמָנוֹת
אֱלֹקִים בִּמְעוֹן קָדְשׁוֹ

*The Father of orphans
and Defender of widows is G-d,
in the abode of His holiness.*

(Tehillim 68:6)

Keeping Life Normal During Aveilus

Q *During the first year of aveilus, what is the fine line between remembering the one who was lost, but still having fun and being carefree?*

A *Aveilus* is hard enough. It is a difficult year. But to become a broken person is not what Chazal intended. A young child has virtually no *aveilus*. However, even with a teenager, if she is having a hard time coping, there are certain adjustments that will be made by any Rav. In short, you should live as normal a life as you can. It is not disrespecting your lost loved one to laugh and have fun with your friends.

No Reason for Guilty Feelings

Q *I am a high school girl and my mother passed away several years ago. One of the things I struggle a lot with is boundaries and guilt. Should I feel guilty if I decide to go* *out with a friend one night instead of making dinner, even if I make dinner every other night? What is the healthy boundary between guilt and being able to enjoy myself and take a break sometimes?*

A girl like you should never feel any guilt whatsoever. You are doing above and beyond what any girl should be doing. You were dealt a difficult situation, and you responded magnificently. The *Ramban* says on the *parashah* of the *Akeidah* that Hashem does not send *nisyonos* to people who cannot handle them. Your history makes it so clear how true this statement is. How you do it is beyond me, but you do it and you should never feel any guilt for the rest of your life!

Proper Way to Honor the Niftar

How can I remember my mother and grieve appropriately if she passed away when I was very young? I don't remember anything. I have no feelings toward her.

When a child under five loses a parent, he cannot be expected to remember much. At the same time, it is even more difficult to grieve if the surviving parent has remarried. No child in this situation should be pushed to grieve.

In general, after the first year of *aveilus*, it is not a mitzvah to grieve. It is a mitzvah to do things so that our departed parent will have an *aliyas neshamah*, such as learning extra, saying more *Tehillim*, giving more *tzedakah*, etc.

Grieving is not what anyone should be doing. We should remember them and to do things so that they will have more *zechusim* in *Olam Haba*. Chazal do tell us that departed parents, or any people who were *niftar*, want to be remembered. That is one of the reasons why we leave a pebble or a stone on their *matzeivah*. But grieving? *Lav davka*.

Setting Boundaries With Surviving Parent

Q I have spoken with Rabbanim about my personal situation and have been told that I need to set clear boundaries with my surviving parent so that I can be normal. However, I still feel guilty that not only am I not going the extra mile for kibbud av va'eim, but I seem to be doing the opposite. How does one balance boundaries and self-care with kibbud av va'eim?

A Before you fly on a plane, one of the travel attendants gives a long speech about safety. One of the things they always say is that if you are traveling with a child and the oxygen masks are ejected, you must first put on your own mask before you assist your child with his.

What about everything we learned about taking care of others first? Well, the answer is obvious. If a passenger stops breathing, neither she nor her child will survive. Only if she is breathing can she help her child.

The same is true in your situation. If you won't have your own life which gives you *some simchas hachaim*, then you will be without oxygen for your parent too. I'm sure you have wonderful *kibbud av va'eim*. You are just experiencing old-fashioned Jewish guilt, and that is not good. You must have a life of your own. If you have that life, you'll be able to help your parent in more ways than you can imagine.

Simchas HaChaim Is Vital

Q My sister says I'm fake because I'm always happy, even though my father passed away. She says that I will struggle in the long run if I'm not sad or upset now. But I don't want to be. I want to just be happy all the time. What's wrong with that?

Your sister is wrong. One of the most important things for *yesomim* or *yesomos* is to find *simchas hachaim*. It took me a while to do so, and I regret the time lost when I could have lived with happiness. My mother tried her hardest to get us to have *simchas hachaim*.

The Pressure Is On

Since my father passed away, I feel a pressure to be super good in school. I'm afraid to cause my mother any grief by not being perfect, but the pressure is getting to me.

You are clearly a young man with *gevaldige kibbud eim*. However, never allow yourself to be pressured, as you will become nervous and anxious and develop stomach-aches and other problems. Your mother, more than anything, wants you to be happy. She does not want you to be perfect, but rather to be a good and happy child. If you get an 85 instead of 100 on a test, she will be fine with that. Yes, mothers want their children to work hard, not to bum around and do nothing with their lives. They want you to *shvitz* a little and do good things. But marks are **not** important. When your mother sees you working hard, she will be very happy. But if you try to make yourself perfect all the time, you will be loaded with anxiety and will be nervous and unhappy.

Just be yourself, and be normal, and work to do well in school. That's all a *Yiddishe mamme* wants. Your mother is normal; she wants you to be normal. She may be a widow and having a hard life, but she wants you to be happy, healthy, and normal.

Still Want to Be a Kid

Q *I am the oldest in my family and I can't figure out how to juggle my parental responsibilities and still be a kid. After my father passed away, my mother really began neglecting a lot of things that need to happen (e.g., shopping, carpools, etc.). I want to help, but I want her to take charge. How do I get her to understand this and step up to the plate without disrespecting her?*

A This is one of the most common issues that *yesomos* face. It is also a very difficult question to answer because every situation is different. I will try to write the general rule. We must do whatever we can to make our surviving parent as comfortable as possible. But you may not allow yourself to be overwhelmed by these duties. If you undertake too much, you will fall apart and will be of no help to anyone. You must have a life of your own, going out with friends and doing all the things a normal teenager does. You are not the parent. Yes, your mother's life is not easy and you must be sympathetic. It might be helpful to bring in outside help to relieve your mother's burden. I also think your school should relieve you of all homework responsibilities. I would also advise you to confide in a morah or rebbi who will speak to your mother to encourage her to step up to the plate and remove some of the burden from your shoulders. It will still be quite a juggle, but somehow, *yesomos* manage.

Treat Him Like Everyone Else

Q *My son, who is a yasom, is in first grade. I wonder if there is any direction being given to the teachers there about dealing with yesomim. Overall, I'm happy with the rebbeim. I feel like they understand my son and deal* *with him pretty well. But I feel like sometimes they are not telling me things because they feel bad for me.*

A In general, schools and rebbeim are very sensitive to *yesomim*. But your son is only in first grade. All this should be left alone. Issues do not come up until fifth or sixth grade at the earliest. These kids are best left unlabeled. No one should think he is any different from the other boys. He should be a regular kid in the classroom.

Train Teachers in Sensitivity

Q *My husband was niftar two years ago and I have a daughter in seventh grade. In my daughter's class last week, a teacher discussed death because it came up in a book they were reading. She asked the girls to discuss shivah and "how long someone should grieve." This is a class full of girls who have never sat shivah. My daughter was terribly upset. When I called the principal about it, I got nowhere.*

We had a similar situation last year in Chumash class when the teacher assigned girls to prepare different pesukim and my daughter was assigned the one about being kind to almanos and yesomim.

I'm not sure why certain topics can't just be skipped, certain conversations avoided, to preserve my daughter's comfort. The school tells me they want my daughter to gain the skills to handle these topics and make peace with her situation. What is the correct derech?

A I don't run your school, but in our yeshivah, on the first day of school, every single rebbi and teacher is told about special cases in his class. They are told to be very sensitive to children from single-parent families. People who are not trained in this area should not discuss the topic with her if it hurts her. I try to work intensively with orphans and widows. I know this *parshah* very well. The teachers you mention are stepping in very dangerous waters. The Torah does not speak kindly about people who hurt *yesomim*, even inadvertently. I know the principal of your school and he is a very fine person. You may share my sentiments with him.

At the same time, it does not have to be the job of the school to teach your daughter how to be comfortable in her own skin. If this becomes an issue, she must see a therapist.

Sensitivity in Teaching Sensitive Subjects

Q *My husband passed away a year ago. I met with my son's rebbi recently and he mentioned that the upcoming piece of Gemara is about yesomim. I asked if it was necessary to teach it and he said it was part of the curriculum. I asked if perhaps it could be skipped in light of the circumstances and he agreed to ask a shailah. What is your opinion?*

A While I am sensitive to the topic, when we skip a piece of Gemara the boys run to learn it on their own, and that can create even more problems. We often have this problem in certain *masechtos*. The rebbi should be able to teach it in a sensitive way and make your son feel comfortable.

However, I do know of a teenager from a divorced home who had a miserable time in yeshivah when they learned *Maseches Gittin*. Not an easy question to resolve.

Sharing the Sad News Embarrasses Me

Q I am eleven years old and my brother is thirteen. My brother tells any person we meet that we lost our father. I cringe every time. I have asked him to stop because I don't think we need to advertise it from the rooftops. What is Rabbi Bender's opinion?

A Everybody feels differently. Some people want sympathy; they want people to feel bad for them. They think that no one understands why it is so hard and that others have it so much better. Then there are those who say they want to be left alone and be treated like a regular guy.

Your older brother seems to be like the first example; he wants sympathy. You are the second type. Everyone is different and while you don't want to do things that way, since your brother does, let him do it his way for himself. If it embarrasses you when you are together, try to work that out with him and ask him not to do it when you are with him. But each one of you is entitled to think and feel as you do and to behave accordingly.

A Guest or a Sympathy Project?

Q For the four years since my father passed away, we have been going to a family friend for Yom Tov. I'm beginning to feel like I'm somebody's "project" and it doesn't feel good. We're still going there, as it's convenient for my family, but it feels so awkward.

A I'm not sure why you feel like a project. There are all kinds of people in *Klal Yisrael*. Some people love to stay home and make their own Yom Tov. Others love to go away. In your situation, it is obviously best to go away. That does not make you a *nebach*. It just makes you someone who will have a nicer Yom Tov if you go away.

Our goal has to be to find happiness during Yom Tov, and the way to find happiness best and easiest is the way to go. It's all in your mind. You have decided that you are a project, so that is why you don't feel good. But if you decide that this is the best thing for you and your family, then you are as healthy and normal as many people who haven't lost a parent and are still going away. Yes, *yesomim* have it harder, but going away does not have to be seen as a problem at all.

Dreading a Dreary Yom Tov

Q *I dread Yom Tov when the table is so empty. Many of my married siblings live overseas or they go for parts of Yom Tov to their in-laws. Even if we go out for a meal, there are still so many hours when it's just me and my mother. I can't even visit my friends because they're all busy with their families. My mother is not the problem; boredom is. And I don't know how to cure it so that I can enjoy Yom Tov.*

A I think it is incredibly important for you and your mother to go out for meals, or even accompany some of your married siblings. Yom Tov is the most difficult time for people who have suffered a loss. I will never forget the first Pesach after my father passed away. We all sat down by the Seder and just kept staring at my father's empty seat. One of my sisters began crying, and it opened up a flood of tears from all of us, until one of us said, "We're here, and we have to celebrate Yom Tov!"

But that does not make it easier for you. You should never be in a *matzav* where you are alone for long periods of time with just your mother. It doesn't matter if you and your mother have a wonderful relationship. Yom Tov is very difficult. Psychologists have written many books about how difficult the holidays are for anyone going through these types of difficulties. It's important that we find ways of combatting the boredom and the sadness. I don't know your exact situation, but I would make every effort to go away for Yom Tov as much as possible, or to explain to your siblings how critically important it is for them to take turns so that there is always a family there with you for Yom Tov.

Hard to Say Yizkor in Shul

Q *I find it very hard to go to shul for Yizkor. Every time I speak about it to other girls in my position, all I hear is, "You can say it at home — it's fine!" I know that's true, but I feel like there's got to be a reason why we go to shul to say Yizkor, and I'm wondering if someone can inspire me to actually do it.*

A I know you don't want to hear that it's okay to say *Yizkor* at home, but I can't argue with the facts. It makes absolutely no difference to Hashem where you say *Yizkor*. You and thousands of other people have a hard time with *Yizkor*. That is perfectly normal! Yes, there is a mitzvah of remembering your parents through *Yizkor*. The way you feel most comfortable is the way you should say *Yizkor*.

As many tragedies as there are, sometimes I look around in my yeshivah and see how many hundreds of people have walked out for *Yizkor*, as is the custom for those whose parents are living. Do I feel jealous? No. I feel good that I can remember my parents the way the Torah wants us to. And the Torah wants us to remember our parents the way we feel most comfortable.

I will end with one word of inspiration. After you do say *Yizkor* in shul together with many fellow Jews, you will have overcome your difficulty, and you will feel much better.

Missing Father's Yom Kippur Berachah

Q Every Erev Yom Kippur, my father used to bentch us and the experience was something really holy, almost surreal. My father passed away suddenly during the winter and I'm so anxious for the coming Yamim Tovim, especially Yom Kippur. I'm going to miss that bentching terribly! Is there anything I can do to try to recreate that atmosphere in the house? Any tefillah I can say and tell my siblings to say?

A As Rosh Yeshivah of a large yeshivah, I have many *yesomim* coming to me for *berachos* on Erev Yom Kippur. I cannot make up for their father or mother, but I can cry with them. Find someone, preferably in your family, whom you love dearly, and have him or her give you a *berachah*. When my father passed away at a young age, my siblings and I all made sure to go to my mother every Erev Yom Kippur to get a *berachah* from her. The tears flowed freely, but it was worth it.

Staying Home on Simchas Torah

Q Since my father's petirah, Simchas Torah is just not a happy day for me. I look down at the dancing from the ladies' section and my father is no longer there and my brothers look like nebach cases. I just wish the day would go away.

A When one loses a family member, Yamim Tovim and Shabbosos are the most difficult times. Yamim Tovim are typically family times, and when there is no father or mother, it hurts the entire Yom Tov. Certainly, there is much potential for sadness on Simchas Torah. But Simchas Torah is not going away. Until you feel better about it, and that day will come *b'ezras Hashem*, on Simchas Torah you can, for the time being, stay home and read. You do not have to go to shul.

Yom Tov Is Too Sad at Home

Q *I am thirteen years old. My father passed away a few years ago. Whenever Yom Tov comes, I have a hard time. Not for myself so much, but because I see my mother getting sad. One Yom Tov, I was at a cousin's house and I was so much happier. I thought of going away this Succos, but I don't want to leave my mother alone. What should I do?*

A This question brings back unbelievably sad memories for me. My father was *niftar* very suddenly. I was fifteen years old, learning in the Philadelphia yeshivah, when Rav Shmuel Kamenetsky woke me up in the morning. Gently and with great compassion and understanding, he told me my father was *niftar* and one of the roshei yeshivah would go to the *levayah* with me. It took me a long time to recover. One thing I will never forget: In the middle of *shivah*, the first Friday night, when we sat down to eat and my father's seat was empty, my mother was crying. Of course she was crying. So we gave her lots and lots of *chizuk*, for she was the one who lost her husband. We, young men, would get married one day and have a full life, but my mother's life ended in a sense that day, though she worked for the next thirty years as a teacher in Bais Yaakov while doing so much for us. But I will never forget that first Friday night.

Even worse was the first Pesach. Pesach should be such a happy time! But as we sat down to the Seder, my father's seat was empty. It was very difficult. My mother was having a very hard time. We, my mother's children, committed that we would take care of her. No matter how hard it was on us, it was harder for her.

So of course, we like to be in happy places, and I understand your feelings, but nothing should come ahead of taking care of your wonderful mother. She is left alone in this world, possibly with very little money, working hard on raising her family and caring for them.

Yom Kippur brings back memories. My mother was very sick for the last many years of her life. I spent five of the last ten Yom Kippurs of her life with her, when she was either in the hospital or ill at home. They were some of the best Yom Kippurs of my life, when I look back on them. I was used to davening in the Mirrer Yeshivah in those days, with an *olam* of over a thousand people screaming out "*Useshuvah, usefillah, utzedakah...*" Yet, instead, there I sat with my mother. What a *zechus*! When I look back now, at first, when she was diagnosed, she was crushed to have become a "sick person," though she tried not to appear sad around us. After a while, she resolved to go on with her teaching and leading our family, and she developed a real *simchas hachaim*. When it comes to Shabbos or Yom Tov, we know that those are the saddest times for people in your situation. Your job is to make your mother less sad.

Purim Is Too Hard Without My Father

Q Purim is very hard for me since my father died because all my friends have these big meals with their families and their father gets high and makes a matzav. We go to an uncle and it's just not the same.

A This question could be asked by someone who is not a *yasom*, too. There are many children who go to family for the *seudah* on Purim or even have a *seudah* at home where no one drinks and it is very quiet and boring. I know in my own neighborhood, there are some who have a big *matzav* and some who don't. Yes, you feel it more because you don't have a father.

But as far as the Purim *seudah* in general goes, some people have some things and some have others. We all have some things that others don't. That's life. Life is like that.

Sometimes, life is not fair when you've lost a parent. I know because I lived it also. My father used to make a big *matzav* on Purim, and when he was *niftar*, the *matzav* went out the window because even if we could have done it on our own, my mother was in no mood to watch the boys enjoying themselves without my father there. So I understand you very well, but you have to accept that in life, it is not the same for everyone.

Now you are going to this uncle who is dry and not exciting. That's life. Life in general. Some are born rich and others have nothing. Some boys wear hand-me-downs their whole life (like I did), while others wear brand-new clothing all the time. Some people have fancy cars and some have old jalopies. Some live in big houses, and some live in tiny apartments and have to climb six flights on Shabbos because they can't use the elevator. That's life. Does it hurt? Sure, but don't think that your problem is a *yasom* problem. Some people have Purim this way and some have it that way. Make the best of it.

I don't know how old you are, but because you want to make a *matzav*, I'm assuming you are about fourteen or fifteen. Maybe you yourself can make the *matzav*! Go out there and make the *matzav* in the house! It doesn't mean drinking. I get very nervous when I see drinking. I've seen a lot of bad things come out of drinking. You want to do what you think everyone else does, but some wives get very angry at their drunk husbands. Some fathers throw up all over their houses. So sometimes a drinking *matzav* is nice, but often they are not so nice.

The bottom line is, count your blessings and let's move on.

Wiped Out at the Seder

Q Last year, I came to the Sedarim like a *shmattah*. I cleaned, I cooked, I served. I cleared. I'm the oldest, and I thought that I had to be the wife and mother that my family lost. It was a disaster on all fronts, as I was angry and explosive all Yom Tov. I learned the hard way, but I wish the Rabbanim would talk about this so that other girls will know that it doesn't have to be this way.

A Your problem of feeling like a *shmattah* is not unique to being a *yesomah*. There are many happily married women who have taken the mitzvah of cleaning and preparing for Pesach to the extreme. By the time they come to the Seder, these women are falling off their feet. They, too, feel like *shmattahs*, but at the same time, they look around the beautiful table and see what their wonderful work has brought them. Sure, it's not your home, but realize what you have accomplished for your wonderful family and take pride in your work.

Rav Pam, *zt"l*, the Rosh Yeshivah of Torah Vodaas, wrote that people always rush to finish the *afikomen* by a certain *zman*, but they forget that it is a major affront to the woman who has worked hard to prepare a wonderful Pesach to rush through things too quickly. Rav Pam explains that it is equally important to enjoy the meal that she has prepared.

The same is true for you. You have put in tremendous effort and prepared a beautiful Yom Tov. Think about what you have done for your family! At the same time, I would urge you not to do this to yourself; not to get to the point where you feel like a *shmattah*. You must find time for yourself. You must buy yourself some nice clothing. You need to look good and come to the Seder feeling happy about who you are. This is directed to the men, too: They should make sure their wives and daughters don't fall apart. They must take care of them and buy them gifts so that they don't feel the way you just described.

Skipping Mah Nishtanah This Year

Q
I'm thirteen and I lost my father close to a year ago. We are going to my grandparents for Pesach and I feel very awkward asking the Mah Nishtanah. I'm sure I will choke up when I say "Tatte leben" and I would rather just skip it. However, I will be the youngest one there. Can I say I'm too old?

A
There's nothing wrong with saying, "I'm not comfortable." Don't say that you are too old, say that this year, you would rather listen to others say it. There are kids who have both parents who don't want to say *Mah Nishtanah* who just tell their parents they are not comfortable saying it and their parents respect that.

However, this is how you feel now, imagining the scene. Once you are there, you will be with your grandparents and mother and other family and will be having a good time. At that point, if it would give your mother a lot of *nachas* if you would say the *Mah Nishtanah*, try to stretch a little bit. You may even say, *Mamme leben*, or *Zeidy leben*, or *Bubbie leben*. But if you can't, you can't. I have no doubt your mother and grandparents will be very understanding.

Share the Task and Go to Shul

Q
Since my mother's petirah, I need to stay home when my father goes to shul on Yom Tov so that I can watch my little siblings, but I really want to go to shul and daven! I feel so connected there! How can I stay home and still feel the kedushah of the day? How can I possibly daven for all my many needs when I'm busy babysitting my little siblings? I feel so torn.

First of all, there is nothing wrong with davening at home. But if you feel strongly that you need to go to shul, then you must work out getting a babysitter to cover for you for at least some of the time. If you ask your mother's friends, I'm sure they will help you out. As important as it is for you to assist your father in any way you can, you must find an outlet for yourself, too. You like going to shul; find a way!

Managing the Pain on Yom Tov

This is my first Pesach without my father and I'm wondering what advice you have to help make the pain manageable. I miss my father!

You are perfectly normal! When we lose someone we love, we're in pain! But that doesn't mean you have to have a painful Yom Tov. I know this will sound cliché, but you know what your father would want. He is in a wonderful place right now. It is us, the survivors, who have the pain. He wants you to have an enjoyable Yom Tov. Is it normal to cry? Of course! But at the same time, it is Yom Tov, and our families need us. You don't explain what your family situation is like, but whoever else is there probably needs *simchah* as much as you do, and together, you will make that *simchah* happen.

Avoiding Painful Reminders at the Seder

As I went through the Haggadah in preparation for my class, I realized that many of the introductions to the simanei haseder revolve around the father. This is obviously very painful for a boy whose parents are divorced and who will be spending the Sedarim with his mother. Should I switch the simanim and instructions that mention the father to something more generic such as, "When we come home from shul, we quickly make Kiddush so the kinderlach don't fall asleep"? I am hesitant to switch this type of thing, as l'maisah, there seems to be a strong mesorah in how this is all done.

A There are two schools of thought in this matter; I personally am not sure which route to take. One school says you should not change anything; we should not run away from the facts. The other school says, adapt to the *yasom* and avoid anything that will hurt him.

My own feeling is a mix of the two. Try to build up the young man in the middle of your presentations. For example, "In your case, Dovid, I'm sure you will help make sure the Seder runs well."

And maybe don't use the words *"Tatte Leben"* before the *Mah Nishtanah*. Give it a lot of time in preparation to avoid what you can avoid.

There is certainly nothing wrong with giving him extra attention.

Inconsistent Shul Behavior

Q *My husband was niftar several months ago. I have five children ranging in age from twelve to twenty-one.*

My twelve-year-old son has gone to shul from the time he was very little. Not because we made him go, but because he wanted to go. My husband was always very careful to be in shul on time. He would NEVER talk in shul. My boys would go to shul with him every day until they reached the age when they have minyan in school. They always behaved, but of course, they were with their father.

Now things have changed SO much. Baruch Hashem, my fourteen- and twelve-year-old sons go nicely to

Shacharis together, but for some reason, my twelve-year-old has stopped attending Minchah and Maariv, always giving a different excuse. My oldest son also told me that my twelve-year-old has been fooling around during Kabbalas Shabbos. Of course, he doesn't like being told what to do by his older brother. He also hardly speaks about his father. He has started going for therapy.

How should I handle this situation?

First of all, I am so sorry for your loss. May *Hakadosh Baruch Hu* take good care of you and your family.

As to your question, leave him alone. We do not know what goes on in the head of a *yasom*. Please compliment him whenever you can. Then, if you must, you may mention, IN A VERY NICE WAY, the things that are bothering you. Most of the time, these problems seem to resolve themselves, especially since he is in therapy.

I know of a *bachur* whose young father died of Covid. The child is a well-behaved *bachur*, learns exceptionally well, and is just a good kid. He refuses to daven for the *amud* or say *Kaddish* in his yeshivah. His mother picked him up every single day, took him to the local *shtiebel* where his father davened, waited for him, and brought him back to yeshivah. We don't understand what goes on in the minds of these children. Our job is, so to say, to hold their hands during this most difficult time. One day, you will be reunited with your husband when that great day of Mashiach arrives.

Lost Out on Spiritual Growth Without My Father

Q *I have a feeling that if my father were still around to raise me, I'd be a better Yid. I feel I lost out on my own growth because I don't have a father.*

There's something called Jewish guilt. It's a terrible thing. I work in a yeshivah with over two thousand six hundred talmidim, *bli ayin hara*, and when *bachurim* become adolescents, they begin to question whether what they are doing is right. Stop! You are a wonderful boy! *Yesomim* often say, "If my father had been around..." Your *father* may have been tougher on you and you may not have liked it. Sometimes fathers demand *Yahadus* and *Yiddishkeit* perfection that puts pressure on their kids. I don't know you, but if you are a little cool and your father would have made you a little less cool, who cares? You are an *ehrliche Yid* who is learning Torah.

Baruch Hashem, you have a mother. You do your best. Hashem does not give us any *nisyonos* that we cannot handle. Your father is in *Shamayim* looking down and admiring his son, the true *ben Torah*. Do you think your father cares exactly what you are wearing? You are wonderful the way you are. Don't worry.

Afraid to Fall Asleep

Q *It's already been a while since my father passed away, but I'm still afraid to go to sleep. I'm scared of the nightmares, and I'm scared of not waking up again, as happened to my father. Is this normal? When will I stop being afraid to go to sleep?*

A This is a common issue. Maybe not very common, but common enough. If possible, your mother should spend time with you at bedtime, even if you are a teenager. This, too, will pass, guaranteed. If a long time passes and you see no improvement, you should see a therapist.

Am I Too Anxious?

Q My husband passed away a few years ago and I have a
son in first grade. His rebbi told me that lately, my son is
spending much more time chatting with him. Recently,
he even chose to skip recess and hang around inside with
the rebbi. I asked my son why he didn't play outside and
he said they were playing a game he doesn't like and
there was nothing to do. I have had a lot of personal
stress in my life in the past few weeks, and I am wondering if I am making my son anxious with all my stress
and it is being reflected in his behavior. Am I reading too
much into this?

A You are over-worrying and it is not good. Kids do their
own thing. They don't have to play ball to enjoy themselves. They don't even have to socialize to enjoy themselves. You should not even ask him why he did not go outside.
You are definitely reading too much into this. I doubt he is anxious because of your stress, but you will make him anxious if you
continue like this.

Can't Stop Crying

Q Does it make sense that I cry all the time at home? I don't
cry in public, but literally everything in my house makes
me cry. (My father passed away suddenly three months
ago.)

A Chazal tell us that the way the brain was originally created, one would never have forgotten anything. But
Hashem saw that one would not be able to go on living
while grieving for a loved one, so He created *shikchah*, forgetting.

Time will heal. For some people earlier, for some later. In the meantime, there is nothing wrong with crying. But you should try slowly but surely to break away from it. It may be healthy and helpful for you to spend time with a social worker or therapist.

Is the Meilitz Yosher Helping Us?

Q Everyone keeps saying that my father should be a "meilitz yosher" for me and my siblings and I keep davening at his kever, but my siblings are going through such a hard time. If my father is looking out for us, why and how are my siblings doing so poorly? It seems that my father doesn't hear me.

A They are not doing poorly; they are having a difficult time. If it goes on for too long, they should see a social worker or therapist. There is nothing wrong with therapy. Your siblings need an injection of sorts. A therapist can help them. Your father IS looking out for you. It may take a while to see it, or you may never see it. But rest assured, he is looking out for you.

Missing My Sister's Support

Q My brother-in-law doesn't want my sister to be involved with our family so much because he feels it's taking away from his family. I'm very resentful because that leaves me, at age fifteen, without her support, both physically and emotionally. He doesn't want her to come over for more than one Shabbos every six weeks, and he doesn't want to do a full Yom Tov because he says they need their space and that my sister is often in a rotten *mood afterward. He has no issue leaving me high and dry. How do I tell him that it's not normal and I'm not okay with this and he has to understand me?*

A Every case is different, but based purely on what you are telling me, your brother-in-law is wrong. When my father passed away, my sister and brother-in-law came to Brooklyn from Lakewood almost every Shabbos for a long period of time. The only way you can handle this is to have your brother-in-law's Rav or close friend advise him that he is in the wrong.

Must I Mention My Late Father?

Q *My father died a few years ago. Now my bar mitzvah is coming up. My mother wants me to mention my father in my speech, but I really don't want to. I'd rather not talk about it that night. Must I do it?*

A Everybody has different types of emotions about a parent who passed away. Some people just don't like talking about it. Some people like talking about it a lot. Somehow, you feel that the night of your bar mitzvah is not a good time to bring it up. On the other hand, your mother, who is a widow, wants her husband's name mentioned. She feels that you, as the *yasom*, should say something nice about him. So let's say you are uncomfortable. I think that once you say it in your speech, and you get it over with and the dancing begins, it will be over and done with. But to please your mother is very, very important, and after all, he was your father. I don't know how long ago your father passed away. I understand that you are uncomfortable. You don't want it to ruin the party. You may even be afraid of crying. I understand all that, but your mother wants it, and everyone there will be expecting it. I'm sure many other speakers will mention your father. When a father is missing from his son's bar mitzvah, it's a normal thing that he is focused on in the speeches. I think it's the right thing to mention him. You have a right to say no, but since your mother wants it, I think it is the right thing to do. On a personal note, the *chasunah* of my first son twenty years ago was seven months after my mother passed away and I cried a lot. It's fine to cry.

How Can I Be Happy?

Q *My mother wanted me to be happy. She said I should be happy even if she dies. I can't, and maybe I won't ever. How disrespectful is that? How mad at me is she? Does she remember what it's like to be down here in this world? I know when we say Shehecheyanu we're supposed to mean it, but I just feel so lost.*

A Your mother understands you perfectly. She was just trying to give you *chizuk*, and permission to be happy. I suggest that you begin working with someone who could use *your* support. When you are helping someone else, you will see that your guilt will dissipate quickly. One thing your mother definitely does not want is for you to feel guilt because of something she told you!

It's Not Laziness

Q *I am fifteen years old and my mother was nifteres when I was thirteen. I have many more responsibilities than the average thirteen-year-old has. Many times, I get lazy about the work I have to do. I come home from a stressful day of school and I'm not in the mood to cook or clean the house. I want to know what can help me stop feeling so lazy. Normally, I have supper around 8:00 or later because I only start taking care of supper when my father gets home. I know it's because of my laziness. What can I do to feel more motivated? It's just so hard to do these things every single day. I want to do it, but I always think, "I'll just chill for a little while and then I'll do it."*

A I think you should do nothing. You are not a lazy person. You are just exhausted and stressed and need to chill. There is nothing wrong with that. You are a human being who just wants to relax a little. A difficult situation was thrown upon you, and you are handling it marvelously. So, you are not perfect. Great. Perfect people get anxiety. Life will go on, even if you don't do everything you want done in the house. Somehow, someway, your siblings and father will manage perfectly well.

My Child Is Afraid of Losing Me, Too

Q *My youngest is an adorable, clever boy of seven. I am planning a short trip to Eretz Yisrael, and last night he asked me if I planned to take him with me. I told him that I probably was not taking anyone. Then he asked me, "If you go, will you die when you come home? Tatty went to Israel and then he died." He added, "Sometimes at night I think about things and worry that you will die." This is the first time he's brought this up. Obviously, I will mention it to his therapist, but is there any message in emunah you think I should give him?*

A The child is understandably fragile right now. If he can stay with family with whom he will feel comfortable, and you call him twice a day, it will be fine. If not, you may want to reconsider taking a trip right now or perhaps you should take your son with you to Eretz Yisrael.

Not Ready to Move On

Q How do I daven for my family to have a nechamah when that means my remaining parent will remarry and I'm not ready to move on?

A *Yesomim* and *yesomos* believe that their lives end when their parents remarry. It is true that sometimes second marriages bring difficulty, but it is also true that second marriages can work out splendidly for both spouses and children. You should daven that your family will have a *nechamah* and that *simchah* should always reign in your home. You then will have your cake and eat it, too.

Rebelling Against Yiddishkeit

Q Since his father died, my eleven-year-old son has been doing things that seem to show an anger toward Yiddishkeit, walking around without his yarmulke, asking for books about different religions, not paying attention during limudei kodesh, only limudei chol, etc. His attitude has improved over the last few months, baruch Hashem, and he has a good mentor and therapist.

Lately, he has been asking me for an iPad. I have explained to him that I won't get something that can be harmful to him. He wants to know if there's anything he can have that would be acceptable. I know there are parental controls for these things, but I'm told smart kids can get around them.

A If you get him an iPad and have it fixed by TAG, you will not have any issues with him circumventing it and you may get him the device. But if you can somehow get away with it, you and your son will be much better off. Technology can ruin people.

Leaving Widowed Mother for a Year in Israel

Q *I am in twelfth grade in a Bais Yaakov school. I am applying to seminary soon and I am not sure whether to go to Eretz Yisrael or stay in New York where I would attend a half-day seminary and work in the afternoon.*

My mother thinks that seminary in Eretz Yisrael would be better for me socially and would be a very valuable experience, though she is not opposed to my staying home either. However, I know that, for her, it would be easier if I stay home so she will not be alone for the year, as my father passed away last year and I am an only child. But she says she wants me to choose whatever I prefer. My principal said that if I am ready to give up my year in Eretz Yisrael to stay with my mother, I will be fulfilling kibbud eim and that will be greater than anything I would gain in Eretz Yisrael. On the other hand, one of my teachers thinks the seminary I am trying to get into in Eretz Yisrael would be amazing for me and that I would do really well there and gain a lot.

I think that Eretz Yisrael would be very good for me, but I will also be happy to stay here and start working. I want to do whatever is better b'ruchniyus and whichever option will be kibbud eim. Which do you think is better?

A You should go to Eretz Yisrael. It will be great for you, and a big *nachas* for your mother eventually. I understand the other considerations and I am a big believer in doing as much as you can for *kibbud eim*, but I still think you should go to Eretz Yisrael.

You should and must prove to yourself that your mother will manage without you, now and when you marry. *Hakadosh Baruch Hu* gives special *kochos* to widows so that they can overcome their difficulties. In your specific case, it is very worthwhile for you to go to Eretz Yisrael.

While I am on my soapbox, I would like to take this opportunity to make it abundantly clear that going to seminary in Eretz Yisrael is not a *mitzvas asei d'Oraisa*. It is very expensive and for some families it can be very difficult financially. You are talking about between twenty and thirty thousand dollars, despite some programs that help. We all understand that the year of seminary in Eretz Yisrael can help a young girl grow dramatically, but they will grow quite well, too, in a seminary in the USA. Don't allow the pressure of others in your community to dictate what you must do.

A Mother's Greatest Nachas

Q *Thank you so much for guiding me and advising me to go to Eretz Yisrael. I am so happy with the decision and that I got into my seminary of choice, baruch Hashem!*

I am really excited to go, but at the same time, I have been feeling so bad about leaving my mother. I'm b'ezras Hashem leaving to seminary in less than two weeks and I feel so torn. I know I will have a great year and I know my mother wants me to go to seminary, yet at the same time, it still doesn't feel right that I am leaving her alone.

A While it may be hard for you and your mother, you are doing the correct thing. You are not the first to ask this question.

You must remember that eventually you will marry and leave

the house. I am sure with your wonderful *middos*, you will visit your mother often. At that point, she will be alone and seriously consider remarrying, which will be the greatest *berachah* for you and her. (Maybe she will consider it this year!)

Right now, the biggest *nachas* for her will be your being *matzliach* in sem. You cannot put your life on hold right now. You must think about your future and that will be the biggest *simchah* for her. I am sure there will be a lot of tears shed in the airport, but once you are gone, she will go about her life.

Agav, most couples also cry when children leave, even without widowhood. Rabbi Zevi Trenk, the *menahel* of our mesivta, married off his oldest child, who moved to Israel. When the young couple went back to Israel after a visit to America for Yom Tov, Rabbi and Rebbetzin Trenk went to the airport to say goodbye. Rabbi Trenk cried so long that he never again went with them to the airport to say goodbye. These are all mixed emotions. In the long term, it will work out wonderfully.

You are a *berachah* for your entire family. I remember your father, *z"l*, very well. He was a special person and I am sure he is having tremendous *nachas* in *Shamayim* from you.

Focus on Seminary

Q *My mother was nifteres when I was fifteen. Now that I'm in seminary and away from home, it's hard not to worry about my siblings. I keep wondering how they're managing. How can I disconnect and still feel that I care for them?*

A One must learn to compartmentalize. Clearly, you have a tremendous personality and you have kept your *simchas hachaim* intact. I am not sure how you do it! There is no reason for you to stop caring. You are clearly the glue that keeps your family together. But at this point in your life, you must focus on your future. Seminary is a preparation for your married years. You will return and begin dating. The one thing I can assure you is that somehow, someway, your siblings will manage. They will pick up the pieces and run with them. Not as well as when you were in the house, perhaps, but they will. Don't forget, the *Avi Yesomim* is watching over all of you.

Including Late Father in the Simchah

Q I wanted to hear what you have to say about including my late father in my simchah as I am engaged to be married. What do I need to know about davening at my father's kever in advance of the wedding? Can I speak to him in English? And what is the mindset? Am I talking to my father or to Hashem? And what can be said about taking this huge step in life without him?

A The Zohar Hakadosh says that fathers and mothers join in their children's *simchah* from the *Olam HaEmes*. Though they are so happy where they are now and do not want to leave, Hashem tells them to come. Rav Nosson Muller recently recounted that he accompanied a thirteen-year-old young man with Down syndrome to his sibling's wedding. When the *chassan* and *kallah* went under the *chuppah*, the young man began to scream, "Ta! Where are you!" and he could not be quieted for the duration of the *chuppah*.

It is incorrect to daven to the *niftar*. We daven only to *Hakadosh Baruch Hu*. What we can do is ask the *niftar* to be a *meilitz yosher*, to beseech Hashem to help ensure you will have a wonderful life. You can say, in any language you choose, "You know how much I love you. I need your help as I embark on my new life. Can you please daven to Hashem to ensure that I have a wonderful home with *shalom bayis*, healthy children, and joy and *nachas*?" Now is the time to tell him how much you miss him and how you wish he were there.

Continuing in Father's Footsteps

Q My father passed away when I was young. My mother remarried right away. My stepfather is worlds apart hashkafically from my father. Now that I am a teen, I'd like to do what my father did. How can I explain this to my mother?

A I think that if you explain this properly to your mother, she will understand you quite well. After all, she was married to your father and she knows exactly what he was like. In her heart of hearts, she probably wants you to continue in your father's footsteps. The challenge may be that she has to have *shalom* and respect for her second husband, so use good judgment in how you present your request. Don't *chas veshalom* put down your stepfather. Just explain to your mother why it's important to you to continue your father's tradition. But the greatest *nachas* you can give your father is to do whatever you can to ensure her happiness, so be sure you never offend your stepfather.

This volume is part of
THE ARTSCROLL® SERIES
an ongoing project of
translations, commentaries and expositions on
Scripture, Mishnah, Talmud, Midrash, Halachah,
liturgy, history, the classic Rabbinic writings,
biographies and thought.

For a brochure of current publications
visit your local Hebrew bookseller
or contact the publisher:

Mesorah Publications, ltd

313 Regina Avenue
Rahway, New Jersey 07065
(718) 921-9000
www.artscroll.com